Report to Parliament

Implementation of the 1985 Changes to the Indian Act

Indian and Northern Affairs Canada
June 1987

 Indian and Northern   Affaires indiennes
Affairs Canada   et du Nord Canada

Published under the authority of the
Hon. Bill McKnight, P.C., M.P.,
Minister of Indian Affairs and
Northern Development,
Ottawa, 1987.

QS-5234-000-BB-A1
Catalogue No. R32-83/1987
ISBN 0-662-55276-8

P9-EDJ-908

The Honourable John A. Fraser, P.C., Q.C., M.P.
Speaker of the House of Commons
OTTAWA, Ontario
K1A 0A6

Dear Mr. Speaker:

Pursuant to section 22 of An Act to Amend the Indian
Act, 1985, c. 27, I am pleased to present this report
to Parliament on the implementation of the 1985
amendments to the Indian Act.

Yours sincerely,

Bill McKnight

EXECUTIVE SUMMARY

It has been two years since Parliament passed Bill C-31 and brought the Indian Act into accord with the provisions of the Canadian Charter of Rights and Freedoms.

Bill C-31 removed sex discrimination clauses from the Indian Act and abolished the concept of enfranchisement. Bill C-31 also provided for the restoration of Indian status and band membership to individuals who had lost them as a result of the discriminatory clauses. Bill C-31 allowed for their children to be recognized as status Indians. In addition, Bill C-31 enabled bands to determine their own membership rules and thus take an important step toward self-government.

With the aid of native associations, individuals across the country have been informed about how Bill C-31 affects them. Many have requested that they be recognized as status Indians. A number of bands have assumed control of their membership, and many others are in the process of developing new membership rules.

Only a small number of individuals have returned to reserves during the first two years of implementation of Bill C-31, resulting in little measurable impact on the lands and resources of bands. Indian and Northern Affairs Canada will continue to monitor the number of individuals returning to reserves. In view of the changes that may take place over the next few years, the department will undertake a detailed evaluation of the impact of the 1985 amendments and present a second report in June 1990.

REPORT TO PARLIAMENT

IMPLEMENTATION OF THE 1985 CHANGES TO THE <u>INDIAN ACT</u>

TABLE OF CONTENTS

LIST OF FIGURES AND TABLES

REPORT TO PARLIAMENT

IMPLEMENTATION OF THE 1985 CHANGES TO THE <u>INDIAN ACT</u>

I. INTRODUCTION

The amendments to the <u>Indian Act</u> passed by Parliament in June 1985 have great significance for Indians in Canada. They represent an end to legislative discrimination on the grounds of sex, which first appeared over one hundred years ago in legislation affecting Indians. In addition, the amendments restore Indian status and band membership rights to people who lost them in the past as a result of that discrimination. Their children are also eligible to have their names entered on the Indian Register. Moreover, in keeping with the government's commitment to Indian self-government, the amendments provide for Indian bands to assume control of their own membership.

Section 22 of the 1985 <u>Indian Act</u> amendments, passed as Bill C-31,* requires a report to Parliament providing the following information:

- the number of people registered under section 6 of the <u>Indian Act</u> and the number entered on each band list under subsection 11(1) of the Act since April 17, 1985;

- the names and number of bands that have assumed control of their own membership under section 10 of the <u>Indian Act</u>; and

- the impact of the amendments on the lands and resources of Indian bands.

Section II of this report describes activities undertaken to administer the amendments. Section III presents information based on applications for registration and restoration of band membership.

----

*   Statutes of Canada, 1985, c. 27. This legislation is cited in the report as "the 1985 <u>Indian Act</u> amendments" or as "Bill C-31".

Section IV examines the development and implementation of band membership rules. Section V deals with the impact of the amendments at the regional and local levels by looking at expenditures on programs and services.

Information on people applying for status is reported as of May 31, 1987. The financial information reflects expenditures as of March 31, 1987.

II. IMPLEMENTATION ACTIVITIES

Implementing the 1985 amendments to the <u>Indian Act</u> has involved making sure that information about the changes is widely disseminated, responding to applications as quickly as possible, and providing additional funding for programs and services. This section discusses the communications activities and the changes that have taken place in the department to administer the Act. Additional program funding is discussed in Section V.

Communications

The news media, Indian and Northern Affairs Canada and native associations all played important roles in disseminating information about the 1985 amendments to the <u>Indian Act</u>. Intensive media coverage of the Bill C-31 initiative was launched by a press conference held on the day the bill was tabled in the House of Commons. National media coverage continued throughout the legislative process and included feature articles in major daily newspapers and coverage on major public affairs programs such as <u>The Journal</u>. Native media also provided day-by-day coverage of parliamentary committee proceedings on the bill and regularly tracked the issue for their audiences.

After the amendments were passed, Indian and Northern Affairs Canada took several steps to make information about them widely available. The department designed and implemented a public communications program to ensure that the people affected were aware of the government initiative and informed about how to qualify for restoration of status and band membership or for first-time registration.

Booklets, posters and information kits were developed to convey this information. More than 160,000 copies of an explanatory booklet have been distributed, mainly to native communities, band chiefs and councils, and native associations. Information was also sent to other interested parties, such as members of the House of Commons and the Senate, libraries, universities, native media, and the general public.

To deal directly with specific inquiries related to the restoration of rights, a toll-free telephone service was established in June 1985. This toll-free number (1-800-567-9605) continues to provide direct access to detailed information from any point in Canada. An average of one hundred calls are handled daily.

The Role of Native Associations

The federal government recognized the important role that native associations could play in facilitating implementation of the amendments. Following passage of the amendments, the department invited proposals from native associations for projects to assist individuals in applying for registration. Since June 1985, one-time grants totalling $3.5 million have been made to eighteen native associations. The associations received the grants to inform those people most likely to be eligible for registration as status Indians under the reinstatement provisions of the Act. Grant recipients are listed in Appendix A.

Responding to Applicants

The success of communications efforts and assistance to individuals by native associations is apparent in the large number of applications for registration under the amended Indian Act. By May 31, 1987 the department had received 43,868 applications requesting registration for 90,051 people. Figure 1 shows the number of applications received each month since the amendments became law.

The number of people applying in the first two years of the implementation period has required several changes within the department. The most visible change has been the evolution of the Membership and Entitlement Directorate.

It was estimated initially that an additional thirty-one person years would be required over a period of five years to handle reinstatement activities. With the high rate of applications, as well as the amount of work involved in their research and investigation, it became clear that more staff would be required. In May 1986 all Indian registration and membership functions were centralized, and person years were reallocated within the department to provide the necessary resources.

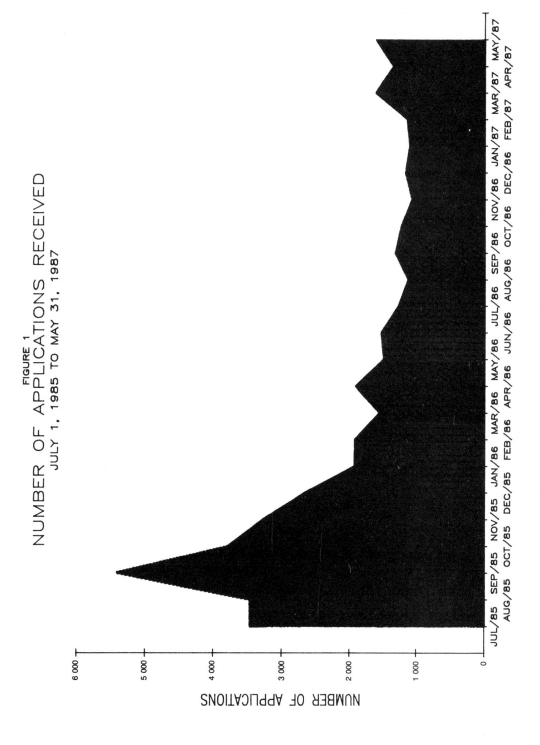

FIGURE 1
NUMBER OF APPLICATIONS RECEIVED
JULY 1, 1985 TO MAY 31, 1987

III. PEOPLE APPLYING FOR REGISTRATION AS STATUS INDIANS

As a result of the 1985 amendments to the Indian Act, any person who lost or was denied status because of the discriminatory sections in the previous law can now apply for registration. The Indian Act provides for an Indian Register maintained by the department, with applications for registration made to the Registrar. Individuals whose names are recorded on this register are considered to have status.

Under the amended Indian Act, those eligible to be registered as status Indians upon application to the Registrar include:

1. women who lost status upon marriage to a non-Indian;

2. individuals who lost or were denied status through other discriminatory clauses in the Indian Act;

3. individuals who lost status through enfranchisement (a process that existed in the old Act whereby a person could give up status in exchange for certain other rights); and

4. children of people in the first three categories.

Determining Eligibility

The Membership and Entitlement Directorate is responsible for determining whether an individual is eligible for registration as a status Indian and entitled to have his or her name entered on a band membership list. Individuals apply to the Registrar at Indian and Northern Affairs Canada, and their eligibility is assessed on the basis of criteria outlined in section 6 of the Indian Act. The process includes searches of the department's records pertaining to the individual and/or to the individual's family.

These records include the Indian Register established
by the 1951 Indian Act. The register records names and
events, such as births, deaths and marriages, of the
individuals registered with a band. If the necessary
information cannot be located in the register, a more
detailed and time-consuming search must be conducted of
the pre-1951 records; these include treaty and annuity
paylists, and archival and census records.

Applications for registration that are incomplete pose
additional difficulties in determining eligibility.
For example, an application might not specify the band
through which the applicant's ancestry can be traced or
might fail to provide information about the
individual's parents that would allow confirmation of
entitlement to Indian status. In these cases, the
applicant must be contacted for additional information
or documentation, such as a birth or marriage
certificate. This often results in long delays before
a decision is made on the application.

- 8 -

Number of People Applying for Registration

As of May 31, 1987 the Membership and Entitlement
Directorate had received requests for the registration
of 90,051 people. Figure 2 compares new requests for
registration with the 1985 registered Indian population
by region.

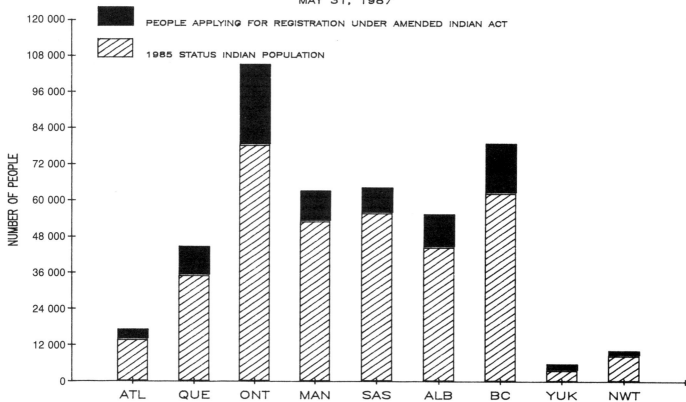

FIGURE 2
NUMBER OF PEOPLE APPLYING FOR REGISTRATION BY REGION
MAY 31, 1987

TOTAL STATUS INDIAN POPULATION = 355 321: PEOPLE APPLYING = 90 051

- 9 -

Of the 90,051 applicants sixty-three per cent have had
their applications considered. Thirty-four per cent of
all applicants have received final decisions about
their eligibility for registration. Twenty-nine per
cent of applicants have had their applications
considered, but additional information from the
applicant or genealogical research is required before a
final decision can be taken. The status of requests
for registration is illustrated in Figure 3.
Applications requiring additional information or
research are shown as being in process.

FIGURE 3
STATUS OF APPLICATION PROCESSING FOR PEOPLE
APPLYING FOR REGISTRATION
MAY 31, 1987

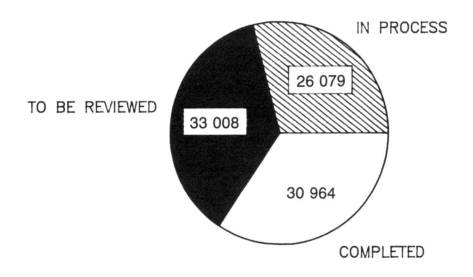

NUMBER OF PEOPLE APPLYING = 90 051

Figure 4 shows the regional distribution of the 24,708
people who had been determined eligible for
registration as a result of the Indian Act amendments
by May 31, 1987.

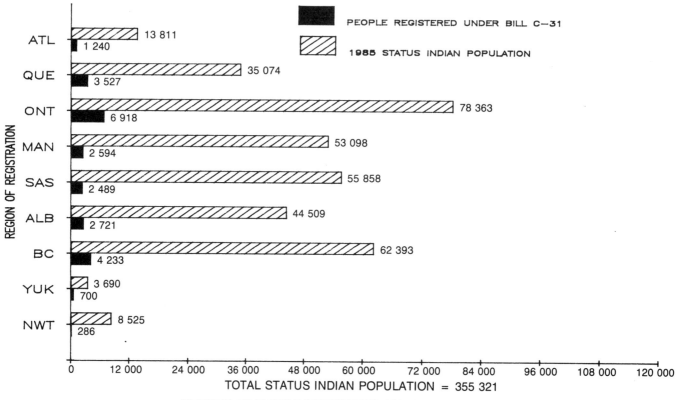

FIGURE 4
REGISTRATIONS COMPLETED BY REGION
MAY 31, 1987

Of the remaining individuals whose applications had been processed by May 31, 1987, there were 1,769 whose names were already recorded on the Indian Register. Another 2,939 individuals have been refused registration. An additional 1,425 applicants' names appeared on more than one application. The remaining 123 individuals had mistakenly addressed applications to the Membership and Entitlement Directorate but were not seeking registration under the new provisions of the Act. These requests were forwarded to the appropriate branch in the department.

Eligibility for Band Membership

Of the 24,708 people newly registered under section 6 as of May 31, 1987, thirty-six per cent were entitled to have their band membership restored immediately under section 11(1) of the Indian Act. The regional distribution of these individuals is presented in Figure 5.

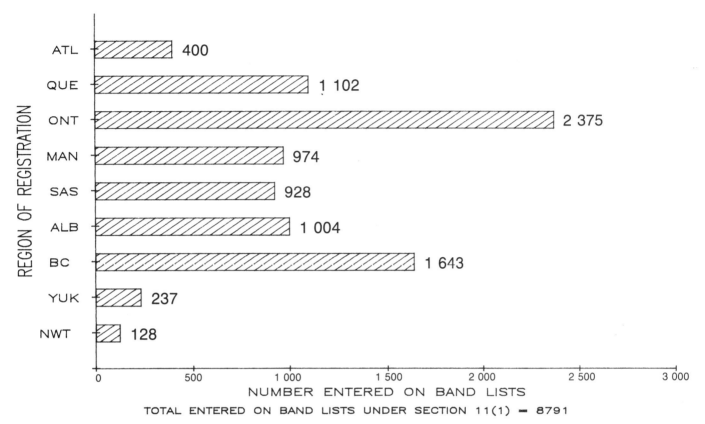

FIGURE 5
NUMBER OF PEOPLE ENTERED ON BAND LISTS
MAY 31, 1987

TOTAL ENTERED ON BAND LISTS UNDER SECTION 11(1) = 8791

In the case of others applying for registration, membership in a band is subject to provisions of section 10 or subsection 11(2) of the Indian Act. During the two-year period ending June 28, 1987, bands may develop membership rules establishing their own criteria for eligibility for band membership. If a band does not act to assume control of its membership within the two-year period, the provisions of the Indian Act will prevail, and most registered individuals will be entitled to membership in a band.

Band-by-Band Statistics

Statistics at the band level, such as the number of people applying for registration, the number of registrations, and the number of people entered on band membership lists, are presented for each band in Appendix B.

IV. DEVELOPMENT OF BAND MEMBERSHIP RULES

The right to determine membership is an important
aspect of self-government, and the 1985 amendments to
the Indian Act provide a means for bands to assume
control of their own membership rules. Section 10 of
the Indian Act sets out how bands may assume control
over their own membership. A majority of electors must
vote in favour of the band assuming control and in
favour of the specific rules the band has developed.
There are also provisions protecting the acquired
rights of existing band members and those eligible to
have membership in their band restored.

The Indian Act allows bands to assume control of their
membership at any time. However, if bands do not act
on this provision and adopt membership rules during the
two-year period ending June 28, 1987, federal
recognition of a person's Indian status will generally
be sufficient to confer band membership on that person.
People who have gained membership in this way will then
have rights that must be respected in any membership
rules a band might adopt in the future.

Responding to Band Initiatives

A total of $6.5 million in federal funds has been set
aside to assist bands in developing and implementing
membership rules. As of May 31, 1987, 490 bands had
requested and received grants to help them develop
their band membership rules (see Figure 6). Funds
distributed to these bands total $3.6 million. In
addition, five bands had received grants totalling
$46,500 to assist them in implementing their rules and
maintaining membership records. Appendix C provides a
list of bands that have received funding to develop
membership rules.

Bands send the membership rules they have developed to
the Minister along with evidence demonstrating approval
by the band electorate. If the rules meet the
requirements of the amended Indian Act concerning the
protection of acquired rights, and if the supporting
documents demonstrate that a majority of electors voted
in favour of the band assuming control and in favour of
the specific rules, the Minister notifies the band of

the transfer of control of its membership. If the new
rules do not satisfy the requirements of section 10 of
the Indian Act, the rules are returned to the band for
appropriate action.

FIGURE 6
**BANDS IN RECEIPT OF FUNDS
FOR DEVELOPMENT OF MEMBERSHIP RULES**
MAY 31, 1987

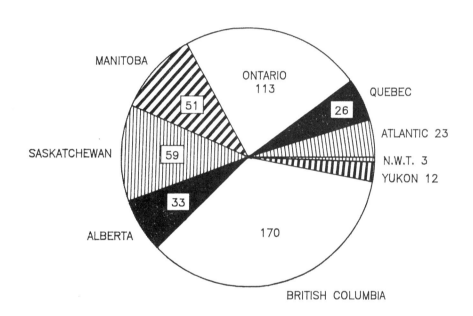

TOTAL NUMBER OF BANDS IN RECEIPT OF FUNDS = 490

Development of Membership Rules

As of May 31, 1987, the Minister had transferred membership control to twelve bands (see Table 1). Documentation has been received from another twenty-nine bands (see Appendix D), and these requests are being reviewed. Three bands have elected to leave control of their membership with the department. Requests for recognition of membership rules can be expected from many of the remaining bands that have received grants to develop their rules.

Table 1

BANDS IN CONTROL OF THEIR MEMBERSHIP

May 31, 1987

Band	Rules in Effect
Sawridge (Alta.)	July 8, 1985
Cumberland House (Sask.)	September 16, 1985
Sechelt (B.C.)	September 19, 1985
Lubicon Lake (Alta.)	February 3, 1986
Swan River (Alta.)	April 4, 1986
Horse Lake (Alta.)	June 3, 1986
Ermineskin (Alta.)	July 2, 1986
Wapekeka (Ont.)	July 15, 1986
Driftpile (Alta.)	November 9, 1986
Saulteau (B.C.)	November 17, 1986
Fort McMurray (Alta.)	January 2, 1987
Chippewas of Georgina Island (Ont.)	February 27, 1987

V. IMPACT ON LANDS AND RESOURCES

The impact of the 1985 amendments to the Indian Act is
being felt in several ways. Newly registered people
intending to move to reserves may affect the provision
of programs and services there. To gauge this
potential impact, the department has reviewed
applications received from bands for additional funds
for programs and services on reserves for these
potential returnees. A second source of information
about the impact of the amendments is individual
applications by newly registered people living
off-reserve, or by people whose bands do not provide a
service they need.

This section provides information on the number of
individuals known to be intending to return to
reserves, as well as on actual increases in program and
service expenditures. Only a small number of people
have returned to reserves to date; as a result, the
full impact of the amendments has yet to be felt. The
department is therefore committed to continuing to
monitor the impact of implementing Bill C-31.

Persons Intending to Return to Reserves

By May 31, 1987, applications received from bands for
additional funds for programs and services for newly
registered individuals showed a total of 1,424 persons
intending to return to reserves by 1990. This
represents a possible increase of less than one per
cent in the total on-reserve Indian population. Table
2 shows the regional distribution of people identified
by bands as intending to return to reserves.

Table 2

NEWLY REGISTERED INDIVIDUALS REPORTED AS INTENDING TO RETURN TO RESERVES

Region	On-reserve Population June 1985	Number of Registered People Reported as Intending to Return May 31, 1987	Number of Bands Requesting Funding for Intended Returnees May 31, 1987
Atlantic	9,985	82	6
Quebec	29,987	193	7
Ontario	53,312	158	13
Manitoba	39,175	290	13
Sask.	36,895	41	8
Alberta	33,532	2	0
B.C.	39,860	469	45
Yukon	2,772	189	11
N.W.T.	7,981	0	0
Canada	253,499	1,424	103

Additional Program Costs

Individuals acquiring Indian status as a result of the 1985 amendments to the Indian Act are eligible for federal programs and services on the same basis as others whose names are on the Indian Register. Whether they live on- or off-reserve, status Indians are eligible for post-secondary education assistance through Indian and Northern Affairs Canada and for non-insured health services through Health and Welfare Canada.

In addition, the federal government provides programs and services to Indians living on reserves much as provincial or municipal governments provide programs and services for other individuals. For people living on-reserve, the federal government provides funds for housing, elementary and secondary education, health services and social assistance, most of which are delivered by bands or tribal councils.

Indian and Northern Affairs Canada is meeting the additional cost of providing these services and programs to people who gained status as a result of the 1985 amendments, whether the services are delivered directly by the department or, more usually, by a band or tribal council. Eligibility and other criteria associated with these programs apply to people with newly acquired status just as they do to others whose names are on the Indian Register.

Program and Service Expenditures:
Indian and Northern Affairs

From July 1, 1985 to March 31, 1987, Indian and Northern Affairs Canada spent $29 million specially allocated for implementing Bill C-31 and providing services to people newly registered as a result of the bill. This consists of $4 million spent in the 1985-86 fiscal year and $25 million spent in 1986-87.

Table 3 presents the Indian and Northern Affairs Canada expenditures related specifically to the 1985 Indian Act amendments in each fiscal year. The bulk has been for post-secondary education assistance, housing subsidies, communications efforts surrounding Bill C-31, and funding for bands developing membership rules. This table shows funding to native organizations to support their efforts to inform and assist individuals eligible for registration and funding to bands to develop and implement their own membership rules. Table 3 also presents Bill C-31 expenditures for community capital facilities. The principal use of these funds has been for water systems, sewers, roads and other infrastructure associated with the construction of houses.

In general, program funding for bands is approved by the department's regional offices; funds are then transferred to bands under contribution agreements. This community-based approach ensures that funds are allocated according to community circumstances. At the same time, to meet the federal government's accountability requirements, the department must receive information verifying two matters from the bands, tribal councils or individuals that have received contributions. First, the people to whom services are provided must be registered. Second, the amounts requested must be reasonable.

The relationship between program and service expenditures resulting from the 1985 amendments and total expenditures for the department's Indian and Inuit Affairs Program is shown in Table 4. Programs and services taken into account include lands, revenues and trusts; elementary and secondary education; post-secondary education; social assistance; welfare services; other education and social services; economic development; band management; capital facilities; housing; policing and administration.

Financial assistance for post-secondary education, provided to 1,730 new registrants under Bill C-31, accounts for six per cent of the department's total expenditures for post-secondary education between July 1, 1985 and March 31, 1987. Subsidies for 347 housing units, resulting from the amendments, represent five per cent of total housing subsidies provided by the department over the same period. Excluding the one-time funding for communications activities and the development and implementation of membership rules, expenditures resulting from the 1985 amendments constitute approximately one per cent of total Indian and Inuit Affairs Program expenditures for the period from July 1, 1985 to March 31, 1987.

TABLE 3

PROGRAM AND SERVICE EXPENDITURES FOR BILL C-31

Source of Expenditure	Expenditures July 1, 1985 to March 31, 1986 ($ 000)	Expenditures April 1, 1986 to March 31, 1987 ($ 000)	Total Expenditures July 1, 1985 to March 31, 1987 ($ 000)
Communications and Membership Rules	3,005	4,056	7,061
Elementary and Secondary Education	0	351	351
Post-Secondary Education	929	8,248	9,176
Social Assistance	0	370	370
Welfare Services	0	11	11
Other Education and Social Assistance	0	11	11
Economic Development	0	17	17
Band Management	37	944	981
Community Capital Facilities	0	2,360	2,360
Housing	0	8,619	8,619
Administration	81	10	91
TOTAL	4,052	24,996	29,047

TABLE 4

EXPENDITURES FOR BILL C-31 AND THE INDIAN AND INUIT AFFAIRS PROGRAM (IIAP)

Source of Expenditure	IIAP Expenditures July 1, 1985 to March 31, 1987 ($ 000)	BILL C-31 Expenditures July 1, 1985 to March 31, 1987 ($ 000)	BILL C-31 Expenditures as a Percentage of Total IIAP Expenditures July 1, 1985 to March 31, 1987 (%)
Lands, Revenue and Trust	61,996	7,061 *	11.39
Elementary and Secondary Education	704,946	351	0.05
Post-Secondary Education	156,048	9,176	5.88
Social Assistance	464,477	370	0.08
Welfare Services	155,043	11	0.01
Other Education and Social Assistance	22,426	11	0.05
Economic Development	160,363	17	0.01
Band Management	224,408	981	0.44
Community Capital Facilities	577,932	2,360	0.41
Housing	182,039	8,619	4.73
Policing	29,021	0	0.00
Administration	143,246	91	0.06
TOTAL	**2,881,944**	**29,047**	**1.01**

* For Bill C-31, this category consists almost entirely of one-time funding for communication activities and the development and implementation of membership rules.

Funding for Test Cases

As of March 31, 1987, $41,000 had been provided for two court cases related to Bill C-31. One case concerns whether the departmental Registrar's decision to add an individual's name to a band list prior to April 17, 1985 can be set aside through protest by band members. The second case concerns the constitutional challenge brought by six Alberta bands with respect to certain amended sections of the Indian Act. In this case, funds have been provided to the Native Council of Canada (Alberta) and to Indian Rights for Indian Women.

Program and Service Expenditures: Health and Welfare Canada

Health and Welfare Canada provides funds for non-insured health services for all registered Indians. These services include transportation, drugs, dental services, eye glasses, health care premiums and contracted health care services. In addition, Health and Welfare Canada ensures access to treatment and health prevention and promotion activities for Indian people living on reserve.

Health and Welfare Canada estimates that per capita expenditures for all status Indians were $395.80 in 1985-86 and $443.40 for 1986-87. Expenditures for new registrants under Bill C-31 are not identified separately. Applying the per capita estimates to the number of new registrants yields total estimated expenditures of $2.5 million for 1985-86 and $9.2 million for 1986-87. Apart from expenditures on non-insured health services, no additional costs have been incurred for the provision of health services to status Indians as a result of the 1985 amendments to the Indian Act.

Measurable Indicators of Future Impacts

Over the next few years, more new registrants can be expected to return to reserves. Thus it is important to continue to evaluate the impact of the 1985 amendments. Areas of potential impact include education, housing, employment, economic development,

health, social assistance, and the availability of
lands and resources (as well as their management).

Indicators of the impact on education on reserves will
include changes in school enrollment. The impact on
housing will be monitored through applications for
housing units and related infrastructure to accommodate
new reserve residents. Employment and economic
development indicators include changes in employment
rates, changes in access to training, and changes in
the demand for lending programs. Changes in health and
social assistance requirements will also be tracked.

It is still too early for the full impact of the 1985
amendments on reserve lands and band resources to be
felt. In view of the changes that may take place over
the next few years, the department will undertake an
evaluation of the impact of the 1985 amendments and
present a report in June 1990. This evaluation will
involve reporting on actual experience with the impact
of the amendments as people return to reserves.

VI. CONCLUSION

The three principles that guided the formulation of the 1985 amendments to the Indian Act were removal of discrimination, restoration of status and membership rights, and increasing the control of Indian bands over their own affairs. With the passage of Bill C-31, the discriminatory clauses were removed from the Indian Act. With respect to the restoration of status and band control of membership, the necessary changes will take time to accomplish. There has been significant progress, however, in the first two years following adoption of the amendments.

The success of communications and information programs can be seen in the fact that 90,051 people have come forward to apply for federal recognition of their Indian heritage. In addition, over four-fifths of all bands in Canada are at various stages in developing their own membership rules. Federal funding has been provided for the additional program costs resulting from the amendments and it is being made available to bands, tribal councils and individuals.

Indian and Northern Affairs Canada is meeting the administrative challenge of handling the large number of registration applications already received. The department will continue to monitor the impact of the amendments on lands and resources and the provision of services and benefits to newly registered individuals.

APPENDIX A

RECIPIENTS OF FUNDING FOR COMMUNICATIONS ACTIVITIES

Association	Amount
Assembly of First Nations	$ 322,528
Association of Métis and Non-Status Indian Associations of Saskatchewan	100,050
Council of Yukon Indians	107,640
Indian Homemakers' Association of B.C.	107,916
Indian Rights for Indian Women	68,770
Métis Association of the Northwest Territories	186,875
Native Alliance of Québec	134,148
Native Council of Canada	257,428
Native Council of Canada, Alberta	121,670
Native Council of Manitoba	150,420
Native Council of Nova Scotia	70,150
Native Council of Prince Edward Island	43,125
Native Women's Association of Canada	1,062,370
New Brunswick Association of Métis and Non-Status Indians	95,220
Ontario Métis and Non-Status Indian Association	287,500
Québec Native Women's Association	138,575
United Native Nations (B.C.)	216,315
Winnipeg Council of Treaty and Status Indians	29,300
TOTAL	$3,500,000

APPENDIX B

BAND-BY-BAND STATISTICS

Introduction

This appendix presents information on the number of people applying for registration under the amended Indian Act as well as the total number of people who have been registered and the number who have had their names entered on a band list in accordance with section 11(1) of the Indian Act, as of May 31, 1987.

The term "unknown band" is used in the listing of band names and refers to people who have applied to the Membership and Entitlement Directorate for registration and have either failed to identify the band to which they are applying for registration or identified the band incorrectly.

Use is made throughout the report of the status Indian population at the time Bill C-31 was passed. This eliminates the possibility that individuals registered as a result of Bill C-31 would be counted twice: once as new registrants and once as members of the base population.

Six Nations of the Grand River is composed of the following 13 bands, which have been listed independently in this appendix:

Bay of Quinte Mohawks	Oneida
Bearfoot Onondaga	Onondaga Clear Sky
Deleware	Tuscarora
Konadaha Seneca	Upper Cayuga
Lower Cayuga	Upper Mohawk
Lower Mohawk	Walker Mohawk
Niharon Dasa Seneca	

When an individual applies to the Six Nations of the Grand River and does not identify one of the specific bands, the individual is listed under the Six Nations of the Grand River. As soon as his or her band is identified, the individual is listed under the appropriate band.

NAME OF BAND	TOTAL APPLICANTS 31/5/87	TOTAL REGISTERED AT 31/5/87	TOTAL ENTERED ON BAND LISTS AT 31/5/87	REGISTERED INDIAN POPULATION JUNE 1985	RESERVE POPULATION JUNE 1985
ATLANTIC					
ABEGWEIT	39	9	5	221	159
ACADIA	227	67	21	386	73
AFTON	56	24	2	253	171
ANNAPOLIS VALLEY	52	18	8	107	60
BEAR RIVER	79	17	8	110	41
BIG COVE	166	58	19	1502	1407
BUCTOUCHE	9	2	0	46	15
BURNT CHURCH	108	49	16	835	709
CHAPEL ISLAND	51	19	8	263	220
EDMUNDSTON	101	30	11	87	71
EEL GROUND	149	57	15	458	308
EEL RIVER	64	14	7	311	209
ESKASONI	110	47	14	1994	1839
FORT FOLLY	9	0	0	47	28
HORTON	46	17	9	82	11
INDIAN ISLAND	23	1	0	79	47
KINGSCLEAR	99	35	14	440	303
LENNOX ISLAND	218	41	14	381	227
MEMBERTOU	115	64	13	500	390
MIAWPUKEK	2	0	0	622	0
MILLBROOK	181	76	16	459	284
OROMOCTO	195	38	14	178	131
PABINEAU	85	30	14	67	51
PICTOU LANDING	47	17	7	318	232
RED BANK	53	26	13	302	263
SAINT MARY'S	212	78	37	548	396
SHUBENACADIE	139	32	13	1100	731
TOBIQUE	394	268	71	894	658
WAGMATCOOK	32	20	5	392	334
WHYCOCOMAGH	12	8	2	482	450
WOODSTOCK	192	78	24	347	167
ATLANTIC - UNKNOWN BANDS	75	0	0	0	0
TOTAL ATLANTIC	3340	1240	400	13811	9985
QUÉBEC					
ABENAKIS DE WOLINAK	143	41	7	83	52
ABITIBIWINNI	69	15	9	485	349
BETSIAMITES	124	46	15	2161	2044
CHISASIBI	133	20	9	1901	1835
EASTMAIN	3	0	0	368	321
GASPE	237	71	17	173	1

NAME OF BAND	TOTAL APPLICANTS 31/5/87	TOTAL REGISTERED AT 31/5/87	TOTAL ENTERED ON BAND LISTS AT 31/5/87	REGISTERED INDIAN POPULATION JUNE 1985	RESERVE POPULATION JUNE 1985
GRAND LAC VICTORIA	25	1	1	266	263
GRANDE RIVIÈRE DE LA BALEINE	4	4	2	417	402
KAHNAWAKE	1051	401	159	5450	5360
KANESATAKE	641	265	74	958	695
KIPAWA	207	64	20	202	139
LAC BARRIÈRE	60	32	8	399	348
LAC SIMON	103	12	7	590	473
LONGUE POINTE	100	29	9	355	231
MANOUANE	26	4	2	1166	1121
MICMACS DE MARIA	234	70	14	554	386
MINGAN	0	0	0	344	334
MISTASSINI	156	80	27	2244	1935
MONTAGNAIS DE NATASHOUAN	21	11	6	469	459
MONTAGNAIS DE SCHEFFERVILLE	42	9	2	493	481
MONTAGNAIS DE SEPT-ILES ET MALIOTENAM	463	144	50	1746	1643
MONTAGNAIS DES ESCOUMINS	250	73	26	144	114
MONTAGNAIS DU LAC ST-JEAN	1303	514	135	2023	1485
NASKAPIS DE SCHEFFERVILLE	9	1	0	396	378
NATION HURONNE WENDAT	1306	637	200	1292	775
NEMASKA	8	2	1	232	229
OBEDJIWAN	16	12	2	1237	1090
ODANAK	451	227	73	696	609
OLD FACTORY	99	20	9	797	704
RESTIGOUCHE	386	128	56	1822	1296
RIVER DESERT	680	226	62	1264	990
ROMAINE	6	0	0	646	645
ST-AUGUSTIN	0	0	0	130	127
TIMISKAMING	653	235	62	479	363
VIGER	96	13	1	125	8
WASKAGANISH	151	44	15	1307	1235
WASWANIPI	119	36	15	920	770
WEYMONTACHIE	55	11	10	694	661
WOLF LAKE	54	19	3	46	20
QUÉBEC - UNKNOWN BANDS	224	4	0	0	0
TOTAL QUÉBEC	9708	3527	1102	35074	29987

ONTARIO

NAME OF BAND	TOTAL APPLICANTS 31/5/87	TOTAL REGISTERED AT 31/5/87	TOTAL ENTERED ON BAND LISTS AT 31/5/87	REGISTERED INDIAN POPULATION JUNE 1985	RESERVE POPULATION JUNE 1985
ALBANY	505	128	36	2011	1354
ALDERVILLE	657	195	33	242	134
AROLAND	14	6	6	226	17
ATTAWAPISKAT	194	55	17	1620	1010
BATCHEWANA	507	124	47	539	385
BAY OF QUINTE MOHAWKS	212	51	10	313	167
BEARFOOT ONONDAGA	67	33	11	311	186
BEARSKIN LAKE	54	10	9	462	389
BEAUSOLEIL	350	114	34	766	551

NAME OF BAND	TOTAL APPLICANTS AT 31/5/87	TOTAL REGISTERED AT 31/5/87	TOTAL ENTERED ON BAND LISTS AT 31/5/87	REGISTERED INDIAN POPULATION JUNE 1985	RESERVE POPULATION JUNE 1985
BIG GRASSY	60	7	2	312	207
BIG ISLAND	55	19	9	229	96
BIG TROUT LAKE	86	20	9	758	735
BRUNSWICK HOUSE	142	35	10	252	104
CALDWELL	16	6	2	79	0
CARIBOU LAKE	51	24	12	520	509
CAT LAKE	0	0	0	377	371
CHAPLEAU CREE	134	28	7	40	5
CHAPLEAU OJIBWAY	7	0	0	22	22
CHIPPEWAS OF GEORGINA ISLAND	247	57	24	237	120
CHIPPEWAS OF KETTLE & STONY POINT	349	114	53	1052	732
CHIPPEWAS OF NAWASH	549	193	50	934	532
CHIPPEWAS OF RAMA	397	94	40	551	369
CHIPPEWAS OF SARNIA	420	164	59	881	524
CHIPPEWAS OF THE THAMES	219	77	34	1229	718
COCKBURN ISLAND	29	2	2	33	6
CONSTANCE LAKE	134	46	15	824	632
COUCHICHING	484	157	55	772	435
CURVE LAKE	467	135	32	811	609
DALLES.	36	6	2	134	44
DEER LAKE	68	12	5	547	521
DELEWARE	139	46	12	340	183
DOKIS	308	79	18	306	166
EAGLE LAKE	53	19	5	182	131
FLYING POST	63	11	3	35	0
FORT HOPE	130	18	10	1246	848
FORT SEVERN	47	11	2	318	289
FORT WILLIAM	300	80	29	556	430
GARDEN RIVER	493	126	41	864	803
GIBSON	284	93	34	253	73
GOLDEN LAKE	483	127	53	585	272
GRASSY NARROWS	70	36	8	689	482
GULL BAY	101	30	12	464	348
HENVEY INLET	85	40	2	209	120
HIAWATHA	223	34	11	150	91
ISLINGTON	41	15	6	901	644
KASABONIKA LAKE	8	3	2	491	483
KEE-WAY-WIN	0	0	0	366	300
KINGFISHER	8	4	0	277	276
KONADAHA SENECA	75	20	8	229	118
LAC DES MILLE LACS	142	48	19	66	3
LAC LA CROIX	10	0	0	246	225
LAC SEUL	229	51	24	1384	664
LANSDOWNE HOUSE	0	0	0	778	178
LONG LAKE NO. 58	254	61	28	638	409
LONG LAKE NO. 77	205	46	24	321	146
LOWER CAYUGA	210	99	35	1711	1145
LOWER MOHAWK	475	184	70	1872	1176
MAGNETAWAN	60	14	4	84	36
MARTIN FALLS	38	9	9	289	203

NAME OF BAND	TOTAL APPLICANTS 31/5/87	TOTAL REGISTERED AT 31/5/87	TOTAL ENTERED ON BAND LISTS AT 31/5/87	REGISTERED INDIAN POPULATION JUNE 1985	RESERVE POPULATION JUNE 1985
MATACHEWAN	192	30	16	156	40
MATTAGAMI	76	11	6	170	103
McDOWELL LAKE	0	0	0	23	23
MICHIPICOTEN	209	24	5	163	49
MISSANABIE CREE	90	22	1	73	3
MISSISSAUGA	274	75	31	406	328
MISSISSAUGAS OF THE CREDIT	329	103	40	744	562
MOHAWKS OF AKWESASNE	675	105	36	4762	4404
MOHAWKS OF THE BAY OF QUINTE	2514	591	187	2822	1355
MOOSE DEER POINT	80	14	9	163	78
MOOSE FACTORY	562	172	48	1646	1097
MORAVIAN OF THE THAMES	185	34	10	556	354
MUNCEYS OF THE THAMES	81	9	6	251	135
MUSKRAT DAM LAKE	13	10	4	214	195
NAICATCHEWENIN	13	2	1	203	173
NEW POST	35	11	2	78	0
NEW SLATE FALLS	3	0	0	81	48
NICICKOUSEMENECANING	11	2	1	121	98
NIHARONDASA SENECA	67	16	6	191	98
NIPIGON	78	13	3	60	42
NIPISSING	131	214	65	694	490
NORTH SPIRIT LAKE	0	0	0	280	240
NORTHWEST ANGLE NO. 33	42	13	5	204	129
NORTHWEST ANGLE NO. 37	84	18	2	133	88
OJIBWAYS OF ONEGAMING	57	7	2	374	250
ONEIDA	256	96	41	979	515
ONEIDAS OF THE THAMES	376	84	27	2736	1425
ONONDAGA CLEAR SKY	62	8	4	369	247
OSNABURGH	81	25	12	838	680
PARRY ISLAND	266	50	16	440	263
PAYS PLAT	82	33	6	92	72
PIC HERON BAY	202	36	13	418	311
PIC MOBERT	179	43	13	403	271
PIKANGIKUM	6	0	0	1180	1127
POPLAR HILL	0	0	0	209	200
RAINY RIVER	86	34	11	513	221
RAT PORTAGE	28	8	5	299	191
RED ROCK	437	146	38	379	144
ROCKY BAY	111	48	21	300	229
SACHIGO LAKE	29	15	5	409	336
SANDPOINT	76	12	1	39	16
SANDY LAKE	12	10	3	1262	1181
SAUGEEN	212	79	26	865	615
SAUGEEN NATION	21	0	0	129	33
SCUGOG	45	4	2	50	23
SEINE RIVER	28	9	5	405	252
SERPENT RIVER	324	91	27	431	219
SHAWANAGA	160	24	10	152	81
SHEGUIANDAH	41	7	3	130	101
SHESHEGWANING	160	24	10	159	110

NAME OF BAND	TOTAL APPLICANTS 31/5/87	TOTAL REGISTERED AT 31/5/87	TOTAL ENTERED ON BAND LISTS AT 31/5/87	REGISTERED INDIAN POPULATION JUNE 1985	RESERVE POPULATION JUNE 1985
SHOAL LAKE NO. 39	53	14	6	316	243
SHOAL LAKE NO. 40	33	9	3	245	144
SIX NATIONS OF THE GRAND RIVER	213	32	15	0	0
SPANISH RIVER	305	53	17	1217	907
STANGECOMING	11	1	1	42	26
SUCKER CREEK	109	6	3	294	236
SUCKER LAKE (FORMER)	7	1	0	0	0
SUMMER BEAVER	0	0	0	269	269
THESSALON	78	11	1	112	54
TIMAGAMI	125	26	11	206	114
TUSCARORA	390	66	34	967	584
UPPER CAYUGA	651	195	11	1378	796
UPPER MOHAWK	1029	342	125	2496	1578
WABAUSKANG	34	6	3	88	19
WABIGOON	87	5	4	164	76
WAHGOSHIG	27	1	0	63	1
WAHNAPITAE	18	2	0	19	9
WALKER MOHAWK	32	9	4	252	163
WALPOLE ISLAND	478	104	57	2156	1623
WAPEKEKA	0	0	0	231	231
WASHAGAMIS BAY	19	6	2	140	102
MAMAKAPEMIN	13	2	2	2	2
WEBEQUIE	8	6	2	460	455
WEENUSK	26	4	1	274	159
WEST BAY	333	92	32	1105	653
WHITEFISH BAY	60	10	4	595	485
WHITEFISH LAKE	198	57	16	291	211
WHITEFISH RIVER	175	45	18	444	271
WHITESAND	80	19	9	432	274
WIKWEMIKONG	936	177	58	3579	2322
MUNNUNWIN	1	0	0	334	330
ONTARIO - UNKNOWN BANDS	569	7	0	0	0
TOTAL ONTARIO	26871	6918	2375	78363	53312

MANITOBA

NAME OF BAND	TOTAL APPLICANTS	TOTAL REGISTERED	TOTAL ENTERED ON BAND LISTS	REGISTERED INDIAN POPULATION	RESERVE POPULATION
BARREN LANDS	245	33	19	363	316
BERENS RIVER	205	48	15	1089	815
BIRDTAIL SIOUX	16	7	2	294	224
BLOODVEIN	47	15	5	571	463
BROKENHEAD	159	64	22	637	195
BUFFALO POINT	38	10	3	34	23
CHEMAWAWIN	182	15	13	528	406
CRANE RIVER	128	28	11	248	136
CROSS LAKE	547	153	44	2562	2136
DAKOTA PLAINS	2	0	0	185	117

NAME OF BAND	TOTAL APPLICANTS 31/5/87	TOTAL REGISTERED AT 31/5/87	TOTAL ENTERED ON BAND LISTS AT 31/5/87	REGISTERED INDIAN POPULATION JUNE 1985	RESERVE POPULATION JUNE 1985
DAKOTA TIPI	19	5	2	171	98
DAUPHIN RIVER	14	1	1	117	99
EBB AND FLOW	158	29	12	825	529
FAIRFORD	204	39	20	1077	793
FISHER RIVER	422	103	45	1441	869
FORT ALEXANDER	551	163	65	3054	1996
FORT CHURCHILL	73	20	11	434	251
FOX LAKE	115	38	11	384	255
GAMBLERS	56	12	2	41	21
GARDEN HILL	39	21	9	1989	1839
GOD'S LAKE	68	44	20	1232	987
GOD'S RIVER	5	0	0	303	293
GRAND RAPIDS	221	54	19	418	299
HOLLOW WATER	155	22	14	580	455
INDIAN BIRCH	14	4	1	167	133
JACKHEAD	47	4	4	357	196
KEESEEKOOWENIN	79	18	8	412	229
LAKE MANITOBA	89	20	15	760	542
LAKE ST. MARTIN	122	42	24	979	524
LITTLE BLACK RIVER	74	17	6	364	256
LITTLE GRAND RAPIDS	74	25	6	1032	902
LITTLE SASKATCHEWAN	109	43	22	402	265
LONG PLAIN	161	52	19	1232	545
MATHIAS COLOMB	118	29	7	1478	1289
MOOSE LAKE	245	13	8	385	341
NELSON HOUSE	420	142	55	2248	2051
NORTHLANDS	15	8	3	481	450
NORWAY HOUSE	495	208	62	2833	2433
OAK LAKE	26	7	3	382	270
OXFORD HOUSE	96	34	14	1213	1134
PEGUIS	979	258	80	2918	1672
PINE CREEK	410	69	28	847	488
POPLAR RIVER	47	17	6	620	591
RED SUCKER LAKE	77	1	1	425	407
ROLLING RIVER	47	14	9	444	259
ROSEAU RIVER	50	26	18	1101	584
SANDY BAY	454	108	36	2260	1695
SHAMATTAWA	64	11	4	656	628
SHOAL RIVER	233	28	8	643	411
SIOUX VALLEY	95	31	15	1220	710
SPLIT LAKE	366	124	29	1378	1142
ST. THERESA POINT	22	13	7	1655	1507
SWAN LAKE	65	23	14	666	255
THE PAS	706	140	46	1566	1359
VALLEY RIVER	129	27	15	569	265
WAR LAKE	3	0	0	82	27
WASAGAMACK	13	6	2	745	710
WATERHEN	171	29	11	515	325
WAYWAYSEECAPPO	96	32	9	1032	601
YORK FACTORY	174	47	14	454	298

NAME OF BAND	TOTAL APPLICANTS 31/5/87	TOTAL REGISTERED AT 31/5/87	TOTAL ENTERED ON BAND LISTS AT 31/5/87	REGISTERED INDIAN POPULATION JUNE 1985	RESERVE POPULATION JUNE 1985
MANITOBA - UNKNOWN BANDS	141	0	0	0	0
TOTAL MANITOBA	10135	2594	974	53098	39175
SASKATCHEWAN					
AHTAHKAKOOP	261	72	29	1412	1113
BEARDY'S AND OKEMASIS	129	52	23	1412	864
BIG C	113	16	7	441	408
BIG RIVER	78	18	10	1366	1174
BLACK LAKE	87	31	8	821	806
BUFFALO RIVER	118	27	9	473	413
CANOE LAKE	267	112	31	549	461
CARRY THE KETTLE	138	56	18	1153	648
COTE	141	54	24	1624	884
COWESSESS	392	90	35	1543	494
CUMBERLAND HOUSE	259	24	6	345	226
DAY STAR	29	7	5	273	143
ENGLISH RIVER	164	68	25	566	478
FISHING LAKE	98	32	11	728	370
FLYING DUST	131	54	15	402	276
FOND DU LAC	125	45	14	829	583
GORDON	263	101	37	1450	961
ISLAND LAKE	13	4	2	533	468
JAMES SMITH	146	42	14	1479	1067
JOHN SMITH	184	54	26	575	380
JOSEPH BIGHEAD	7	2	0	433	351
KAHKEWISTAHAW	121	24	6	750	291
KEESEEKOOSE	131	31	18	959	465
KEY	97	22	11	560	173
KINISTINO	38	6	5	474	284
LAC LA HACHE	123	32	8	470	452
LAC LA RONGE	594	178	75	3221	2801
LITTLE BLACK BEAR	28	16	9	233	110
LITTLE PINE	55	25	11	988	576
LUCKY MAN	5	2	1	64	20
MAKWA SAHGAIEHCAN	12	3	3	662	534
MISTAWASIS	194	49	19	1031	559
MONTREAL LAKE	144	46	22	1469	1158
MOOSE WOODS	24	12	3	199	135
MOOSOMIN	104	34	8	706	458
MOSQUITO - GRIZZLY BEAR'S HEAD	16	6	2	685	433
MUSCOMPETUNG	151	41	13	642	325
MUSKEG LAKE	249	74	32	703	320
MUSKOWEKWAN	75	23	11	681	385
NIKANEET	17	0	0	181	111

NAME OF BAND	TOTAL APPLICANTS 31/5/87	TOTAL REGISTERED AT 31/5/87	TOTAL ENTERED ON BAND LISTS AT 31/5/87	REGISTERED INDIAN POPULATION JUNE 1985	RESERVE POPULATION JUNE 1985
NUT LAKE	44	6	3	1368	683
OCHAPOWACE	115	30	12	660	284
OKANESE	62	11	7	266	137
ONE ARROW	31	9	5	673	370
ONION LAKE	219	80	38	1867	1496
PASQUA	125	56	12	821	414
PEEPEEKISIS	267	141	40	1153	633
PELICAN LAKE	56	9	6	503	463
PETER BALLANTYNE	582	107	35	2735	2509
PIAPOT	51	14	6	980	432
POORMAN	39	6	4	1299	707
POUNDMAKER	62	26	11	705	460
RED EARTH	53	13	5	573	536
RED PHEASANT	228	77	13	847	468
SAKIMAY	141	37	18	722	189
SAULTEAUX	33	12	3	543	331
SHOAL LAKE OF THE CREE NATION	32	3	1	320	314
STANDING BUFFALO	58	23	8	689	384
STAR BLANKET	25	17	9	255	130
STURGEON LAKE	106	30	14	1145	915
SWEET GRASS	100	28	9	810	471
THUNDERCHILD	70	31	7	1119	614
TURNOR LAKE	75	19	6	159	148
WAHPETON	36	29	13	140	131
WATERHEN LAKE	111	20	8	788	525
WHITE BEAR	144	59	28	1389	730
MITCHEKAN LAKE	11	0	0	298	228
WOOD MOUNTAIN	60	7	4	78	35
SASKATCHEWAN - UNKNOWN BANDS	138	1	0	0	0
TOTAL SASKATCHEWAN	8434	2489	928	55858	36895

ALBERTA

ALEXANDER	230	57	24	752	565
ALEXIS	85	27	8	761	558
BEAVER LAKE	219	44	19	320	236
BIGSTONE CREE	952	179	91	2073	1570
BLACKFOOT	217	103	37	3308	2174
BLOOD	294	119	49	6322	5256
BOYER RIVER	96	20	8	333	205
COLD LAKE FIRST NATIONS	396	118	56	1078	694
CREE	228	52	19	1071	622
DENE THA'	158	64	26	1444	1236
DRIFTPILE	453	100	39	816	453
DUNCAN'S	54	2	2	63	42
ENOCH	219	101	34	907	732

NAME OF BAND	TOTAL APPLICANTS 31/5/87	TOTAL REGISTERED AT 31/5/87	TOTAL ENTERED ON BAND LISTS AT 31/5/87	REGISTERED INDIAN POPULATION JUNE 1985	RESERVE POPULATION JUNE 1985
ERMINESKIN	292	102	38	1598	1292
FORT CHIPEWYAN	311	27	12	327	195
FORT McKAY	96	28	7	235	140
FORT McMURRAY	170	36	11	154	38
FROG LAKE	125	43	13	995	745
GROUARD	55	9	4	91	47
HEART LAKE	54	3	3	101	63
HORSE LAKE	238	22	9	194	127
JANVIER	67	19	10	278	188
KEHEWIN	141	39	14	907	695
LITTLE RED RIVER	150	45	13	1601	1427
LOUIS BULL	23	9	7	799	609
LUBICON LAKE	44	4	1	191	116
MICHEL (FORMER)	567	131	0	0	0
MONTANA	466	11	3	449	324
O'CHIESE	37	10	7	381	308
PAUL	72	28	9	914	656
PEIGAN	165	46	22	1977	1491
SADDLE LAKE	935	483	182	4206	2982
SAMSON	287	133	46	3069	2484
SARCEE	145	37	14	738	673
SAWRIDGE	324	43	6	38	18
STONEY (BEARSPAW)	1	0	0	826	792
STONEY (CHINIKI)	3	2	1	829	808
STONEY (GOODSTONEY)	6	5	2	881	827
STURGEON LAKE	447	50	26	887	551
SUCKER CREEK	586	155	49	715	335
SUNCHILD CREE	20	4	2	491	336
SWAN RIVER	369	65	20	277	131
TALLCREE	190	43	12	388	276
WHITEFISH LAKE	501	97	43	706	503
ALBERTA - UNKNOWN BANDS	511	6	0	0	0
TOTAL ALBERTA	11008	2721	1004	44509	33532

BRITISH COLUMBIA

NAME OF BAND	TOTAL APPLICANTS 31/5/87	TOTAL REGISTERED AT 31/5/87	TOTAL ENTERED ON BAND LISTS AT 31/5/87	REGISTERED INDIAN POPULATION JUNE 1985	RESERVE POPULATION JUNE 1985
ADAMS LAKE	71	15	9	395	311
AHOUSAHT	99	30	14	1097	564
AITCHELITZ	0	0	0	18	18
ALEXANDRIA	56	14	1	64	43
ALEXIS CREEK	31	5	3	443	347
ALKALI LAKE	71	17	6	406	351
ANAHAM	78	34	15	832	637
ANDERSON LAKE	60	8	4	141	78
ASHCROFT	88	33	8	85	44
BECHER BAY	23	11	2	137	77

NAME OF BAND	TOTAL APPLICANTS 31/5/87	TOTAL REGISTERED AT 31/5/87	TOTAL ENTERED ON BAND LISTS AT 31/5/87	REGISTERED INDIAN POPULATION JUNE 1985	RESERVE POPULATION JUNE 1985
BELLA COOLA	122	27	16	851	620
BLUEBERRY RIVER	34	11	3	171	120
BONAPARTE	117	10	7	406	180
BOOTHROYD	28	2	1	181	94
BOSTON BAR	96	10	0	103	69
BRIDGE RIVER	36	4	4	207	111
BROMAN LAKE	20	10	2	102	56
BURNS LAKE	47	3	1	33	26
BURRARD	88	15	10	168	145
CAMPBELL RIVER	158	69	25	247	115
CANIM LAKE	24	1	0	360	307
CANOE CREEK	51	12	3	314	174
CANYON CITY	54	5	2	211	123
CAPE MUDGE	209	80	32	436	307
CAYOOSE CREEK	11	0	0	113	84
CHEAM	74	39	11	197	138
CHEHALIS	123	32	14	506	332
CHEMAINUS	78	25	11	600	489
CHESLATTA	22	3	2	149	101
CLAYOQUOT	23	3	1	461	247
COLDWATER	99	6	3	340	232
COLUMBIA LAKE	20	3	2	146	88
COMOX	83	38	13	92	66
COOK'S FERRY	64	26	10	171	88
COQUITLAM	25	0	0	18	4
COWICHAN	192	46	25	2069	1535
COWICHAN LAKE	5	1	0	8	8
DITIDAHT	31	11	5	284	137
DOIG RIVER	16	6	2	141	110
DOUGLAS	24	7	3	133	55
EHATTESAHT	4	0	0	118	19
ESQUIMALT	14	1	1	92	51
FORT GEORGE	122	20	11	93	89
FORT NELSON	101	35	19	359	253
FORT WARE	47	3	2	222	175
FOUNTAIN	67	11	4	566	364
FRASER LAKE	41	9	2	211	158
GITANMAAX	479	128	52	935	550
GITLAKDAMIX	148	50	21	1115	694
GITWANGAK	179	47	14	533	343
GLEN VOWELL	78	15	5	228	126
GWA'SALA - NAKWAXDA'XW	8	2	1	375	352
HAGWILGET	203	53	9	284	158
HALALT	11	9	2	142	72
HALFWAY RIVER	9	0	0	138	118
HARTLEY BAY	121	48	16	461	242
HEILTSUK	179	76	34	1385	1257
HESQUIAHT	20	0	0	423	52
HIGH BAR	67	1	0	9	0
HOMALCO	55	13	4	226	95

NAME OF BAND	TOTAL APPLICANTS 31/5/87	TOTAL REGISTERED AT 31/5/87	TOTAL ENTERED ON BAND LISTS AT 31/5/87	REGISTERED INDIAN POPULATION JUNE 1985	RESERVE POPULATION JUNE 1985
HOPE	47	1	1	195	89
INGENIKA	8	2	2	201	160
ISKUT	38	11	5	357	234
KAMLOOPS	168	37	17	481	347
KANAKA BAR	43	10	5	76	32
KATZIE	69	18	8	210	145
KINCOLITH	318	61	20	1112	420
KISPIOX	256	78	33	739	431
KITIMAAT	192	55	30	1062	644
KITASOO	15	2	1	311	265
KITKATLA	144	33	13	1006	497
KITSEGUKLA	135	52	19	498	360
KITSELAS	166	36	6	118	47
KITSUMKALUM	342	41	11	142	77
KITWANCOOL	55	20	6	373	276
KLAHOOSE	80	12	6	101	33
KLUSKUS	3	0	0	127	91
KWAKIUTL	90	32	10	296	141
KWAW-KWAW-A-PILT	0	0	0	25	16
KWA-WA-AINEUK	0	0	0	21	21
KWIAKAH	1	0	0	13	9
KWICKSUTAINEUK-AH-KWAW-AH-MISH	34	15	4	191	67
KYUQUOT	42	12	3	274	191
LAKAHAHMEN	111	13	6	118	42
LAKALZAP	77	15	8	940	382
LAKE BABINE	166	49	11	1114	801
LANGLEY	11	0	0	75	53
LAX KW'ALAAMS	491	197	54	1610	906
LILLOOET	81	15	9	133	88
LITTLE SHUSWAP LAKE	39	11	8	195	154
LOWER KOOTENAY	9	1	1	99	81
LOWER NICOLA	154	36	12	440	315
LOWER SIMILKAMEEN	59	24	9	229	178
LYACKSON	32	10	9	101	21
LYTTON	245	69	39	1082	765
MALAHAT	1	0	0	179	111
MAMALELEQALLA-QWE'QWA'SOT'ENOX	35	21	11	213	49
MASSET	695	183	50	1248	625
MATSQUI	29	10	2	61	26
McLEOD LAKE	45	8	3	241	87
METLAKATLA	221	57	12	275	124
MORICETOWN	292	86	19	787	480
MOUNT CURRIE	60	17	5	1169	830
MOWACHAHT	8	5	1	306	163
MUSQUEAM	169	56	25	541	382
NANAIMO	163	43	21	658	424
NANOOSE	9	1	0	135	80
NAZKO	25	5	4	191	147
NECOSLIE	245	63	21	751	470
NEE-TAHI-BUHN	32	6	5	126	72

NAME OF BAND	TOTAL APPLICANTS 31/5/87	TOTAL REGISTERED AT 31/5/87	TOTAL ENTERED ON BAND LISTS AT 31/5/87	REGISTERED INDIAN POPULATION JUNE 1985	RESERVE POPULATION JUNE 1985
NEMAIAH VALLEY	11	6	3	255	221
NESKAINLITH	84	12	9	354	231
NEW WESTMINSTER	0	0	0	2	0
NICOMEN	6	0	0	68	40
NIMPKISH	280	110	38	959	633
NOOAITCH	15	7	2	106	63
NORTH THOMPSON	102	18	8	355	179
NUCHATLAHT	0	0	0	68	41
OHAMIL	29	2	2	65	25
OHIAHT	28	12	4	335	101
OKANAGAN	354	144	58	895	603
OPETCHESAHT	33	22	11	120	56
OREGON JACK CREEK	3	1	1	26	11
OSOYOOS	43	7	3	175	158
OWEEKENO	41	7	3	152	65
PACHEENAHT	20	5	3	173	66
PAUQUACHIN	9	2	1	203	160
PAVILION	58	15	5	264	211
PENELAKUT	70	8	3	478	292
PENTICTON	94	20	12	391	303
PETERS	33	11	5	40	29
POPKUM	4	0	0	7	7
PROPHET RIVER	4	1	0	130	88
QUALICUM	20	1	1	47	37
QUATSINO	15	2	2	187	140
QUESNEL	77	1	1	68	59
SAMAHQUAM	31	7	3	154	1
SAULTEAU	160	29	14	203	135
SCOWLITZ	3	0	0	167	90
SEABIRD ISLAND	49	2	2	371	247
SECHELT	133	27	18	644	414
SEMIAHMOO	39	11	4	28	24
SETON LAKE	30	1	1	408	302
SHACKAN	8	3	1	92	54
SHESHAHT	64	40	13	517	436
SHUSWAP	44	3	2	150	99
SISKA	37	1	0	117	43
SKAWAHLOOK	5	0	0	54	16
SKEETCHESTN	77	14	7	253	134
SKIDEGATE	560	163	59	468	249
SKOOKUM CHUCK	38	9	9	230	28
SKOWKALE	8	0	0	94	69
SKUPPAH	28	5	3	31	18
SKWAH	68	9	5	263	141
SKWAY	25	2	2	46	11
SLIAMMON	57	13	12	518	443
SODA CREEK	48	13	9	173	121
SONGHEES	23	11	4	214	154
SOOKE	41	7	4	50	25
SOOWAHLIE	32	6	4	161	80

NAME OF BAND	TOTAL APPLICANTS AT 31/5/87	TOTAL REGISTERED AT 31/5/87	TOTAL ENTERED ON BAND LISTS AT 31/5/87	REGISTERED INDIAN POPULATION JUNE 1985	RESERVE POPULATION JUNE 1985
SPALLUMCHEEN	68	21	10	378	257
SPUZZUM	84	20	2	49	17
SQUAMISH	658	188	68	1531	1335
SQUIALA	5	0	0	71	48
STELLAQUO	108	13	4	206	154
STONE	4	1	1	210	186
STONY CREEK	66	29	10	463	356
STUART - TREMBLEUR LAKE	129	25	11	978	694
ST. MARY'S	59	13	2	152	108
SUMAS	43	18	6	136	109
TAHLTAN	653	125	33	534	185
TAKLA LAKE	73	11	3	385	274
TANAKTEUK	26	3	3	110	13
TLATLASIKWALA	0	0	0	27	10
TLOWITSIS - MUMTAGILA	26	5	3	172	51
TOBACCO PLAINS	33	2	1	87	75
TOOSEY	22	12	4	129	89
TOQUAHT	13	9	3	74	11
TSARLIP	47	4	4	455	349
TSAWATAINEUK	73	21	7	308	118
TSAWOUT	70	15	6	359	265
TSAWWASSEN	79	26	9	63	44
TSEYCUM	17	5	4	101	61
TZEACHTEN	73	20	6	138	103
UCHUCKLESAHT	5	3	1	108	17
UCLUELET	35	10	3	396	274
ULKATCHO	56	12	5	419	331
UNION BAR	45	4	1	49	12
UPPER NICOLA	148	40	20	472	331
UPPER SIMILKAMEEN	6	0	0	30	23
WEST MOBERLY LAKE	24	2	1	72	26
WESTBANK	64	34	18	242	206
WHISPERING PINES	21	3	2	47	40
WILLIAMS LAKE	87	10	8	267	178
YAKWEAKWIOOSE	4	0	0	25	19
YALE	24	0	0	91	39
BRITISH COLUMBIA - UNKNOWN BANDS	324	2	0	0	0
TOTAL BRITISH COLUMBIA	16582	4233	1643	62393	39860

NORTHWEST TERRITORIES

NAME OF BAND	TOTAL APPLICANTS AT 31/5/87	TOTAL REGISTERED AT 31/5/87	TOTAL ENTERED ON BAND LISTS AT 31/5/87	REGISTERED INDIAN POPULATION JUNE 1985	RESERVE POPULATION JUNE 1985
AKLAVIK	56	12	6	248	239
ARCTIC RED RIVER	75	14	6	253	239
DOG RIB RAE	147	31	91	1811	1748
FITZ-SMITH (ALTA - NWT) NATIVE	168	20	8	368	334

NAME OF BAND	TOTAL APPLICANTS 31/5/87	TOTAL REGISTERED AT 31/5/87	TOTAL ENTERED ON BAND LISTS AT 31/5/87	REGISTERED INDIAN POPULATION JUNE 1985	RESERVE POPULATION JUNE 1985
FORT FRANKLIN	45	16	8	546	527
FORT GOOD HOPE	107	19	5	482	473
FORT LIARD	54	4	4	493	479
FORT McPHERSON	302	67	30	724	701
FORT NORMAN	115	13	3	236	228
FORT PROVIDENCE	76	15	5	630	580
FORT SIMPSON	130	34	11	762	725
FORT WRIGLEY	29	9	7	216	211
HAY RIVER	64	5	3	303	283
INUVIK NATIVE	20	0	0	94	2
RESOLUTION	143	6	3	380	345
SNOWDRIFT	28	5	1	331	292
YELLOWKNIFE 'B'	74	16	6	648	575
NWT - UNKNOWN BANDS	57	0	0	0	0
TOTAL NORTHWEST TERRITORIES	1690	286	128	8525	7981
YUKON					
AISHIHIK	46	25	10	86	56
CARCROSS-TAGISH	220	61	12	145	104
CHAMPAGNE	186	66	24	175	105
DAWSON	194	66	22	222	131
KLUANE	163	38	10	110	80
KWANLIN DUN	313	140	34	543	482
LIARD RIVER	140	34	15	620	474
LITTLE SALMON - CARMACKS	85	31	13	301	228
NA-CHO NY'A'K-DUN	122	63	29	224	204
OLD CROW	113	51	18	236	179
ROSS RIVER	36	20	8	289	270
SELKIRK	172	21	10	287	169
TAKU RIVER TLINGIT	159	33	11	187	73
TESLIN	171	51	21	265	211
TOTAL YUKON	2120	700	237	3690	2772
REGION - UNKNOWN BANDS	163	0	0	0	0
TOTAL CANADA	90051	24708	8791	355321	2534499

APPENDIX C

BANDS AND ASSOCIATIONS IN RECEIPT OF FUNDING FOR
THE DEVELOPMENT OF MEMBERSHIP RULES, MAY 31, 1987

The total funding provided to bands and associations for the development of membership rules was $3,604,272 as of May 31, 1987.

The regional distribution of these funds was as follows:

ATLANTIC REGION   **TOTAL FUNDING PROVIDED:** $163,500

BANDS RECEIVING FUNDS:

ABEGWEIT	EEL GROUND	OROMOCTO
ANNAPOLIS VALLEY	EEL RIVER	PAPINEAU
BIG COVE	ESKASONI	RED BANK
BUCTOUCHE	FORT FOLLY	SAINT MARY'S
BURNT CHURCH	INDIAN ISLAND	SHUBENACADIE
CHAPEL ISLAND	LENNOX ISLAND	WAGMATCOOK
EDMUNDSTON	MILLBROOK	WHYCOCOMAGH
		WOODSTOCK

QUEBEC REGION   **TOTAL FUNDING PROVIDED:** $187,900

BANDS RECEIVING FUNDS:

ABENAKIS DE WOLINAK	MONTAGNAIS DE SEPT-ÎLES ET
ABITIBIWINNI	MALIOTENAM
BETSIAMITES	MONTAGNAIS DE NATASHQUAN
GASPE	MONTAGNAIS DU LAC ST. JEAN
KAHNAWAKE	NATION HURONNE WENDAT
KANESATAKE	OBEDJIWAN
KIPAWA	ODANAK
LAC SIMON	RESTIGOUCHE
LONG POINT	RIVER DESERT
MANOUANE	TIMISKAMING
MICMACS DE MARIA	WEYMONTACHIE
MINGAN	WOLF LAKE

APPENDIX C

BANDS AND ASSOCIATIONS IN RECEIPT OF FUNDING FOR
THE DEVELOPMENT OF MEMBERSHIP RULES, MAY 31, 1987

ONTARIO REGION   TOTAL FUNDING PROVIDED: $776,392

BANDS RECEIVING FUNDS:

ALDERVILLE   MOHAWKS OF THE BAY OF QUINTE
AROLUND   MOOSE DEER POINT
BEAUSOLEIL   MOOSE FACTORY
BIG GRASSY   MUNCEYS OF THE THAMES
BIG ISLAND   NAICATCHEWENIN
BIG TROUT LAKE   NICICKOUSEMENECANING
CALDWELL   NIPISSING
CHIPPEWAS OF GEORGINA ISLAND   NORTHWEST ANGLE NO. 33
CHIPPEWAS OF KETTLE & STONY POINT   NORTHWEST ANGLE NO. 37
CHIPPEWAS OF NAWASH   OJIBWAYS OF ONEGAMING
CHIPPEWAS OF RAMA   ONEIDAS OF THE THAMES
CHIPPEWAS OF SARNIA   PARRY ISLAND
CHIPPEWAS OF THE THAMES   PAYS PLAT
COCKBURN ISLAND   PIC HERON BAY
CONSTANCE LAKE   PIC MOBERT
COUCHICHING   PIKANGIKUM
CURVE LAKE   RAINY RIVER
DALLES   RAT PORTAGE
DEER LAKE   ROCKY BAY
DOKIS   SANDPOINT
EAGLE LAKE   SCUGOG
FORT HOPE   SEINE RIVER
FORT WILLIAM   SHAWANAGA
GARDEN RIVER   SHEGUIANDAH
GIBSON   SHOAL LAKE NO. 39
GRASSY NARROWS   SIX NATIONS OF THE GRAND RIVER
GULL BAY   STANGECOMING
HENVEY INLET   SUCKER CREEK
HIAWATHA   WABIGOON
ISLINGTON   WAHCOSHIG
LAC DES MILLE LACS   WAHNAPITAE
LAC LA CROIX   WALPOLE ISLAND
LAC SEUL   WAPEKEKA
LONG LAKE NO. 58   WASHAGAMIS BAY
LONG LAKE NO. 77   WHITEFISH BAY
MAGNETAWAN   WHITEFISH RIVER
MISSISSAUGA   WHITESAND
MISSISSAUGA OF THE CREDIT   WIKWEMIKONG
MOHAWKS OF AKWESASNE

NATIVE ASSOCIATIONS RECEIVING FUNDS:

NORTH SHORE TRIBAL COUNCIL   SHIBOGAMA TRIBAL COUNCIL
PEHTABUN AREA COUNCIL   WINDIGO AREA COUNCIL

APPENDIX C

BANDS AND ASSOCIATIONS IN RECEIPT OF FUNDING FOR THE DEVELOPMENT OF MEMBERSHIP RULES, MAY 31, 1987

MANITOBA REGION   **TOTAL FUNDING PROVIDED:** $309,100

BANDS RECEIVING FUNDS:

BARREN LANDS	LAKE MANITOBA	ROSEAU RIVER
CRANE RIVER	LAKE ST. MARTIN	SANDY BAY
CROSS LAKE	LITTLE SASKATCHEWAN	SIOUX VALLEY
DAKOTA TIPI	LONG PLAIN	SPLIT LAKE
EBB AND FLOW	NELSON HOUSE	SWAN LAKE
FAIRFORD	NORWAY HOUSE	VALLEY RIVER
FISHER RIVER	OAK LAKE	WATERHEN
FORT ALEXANDER	OXFORD HOUSE	WAYWAYSEECAPPO
GAMBLERS	PEGUIS	WASAGAMACK
GOD'S LAKE	PINE CREEK	YORK FACTORY

NATIVE ASSOCIATIONS RECEIVING FUNDING:

SOUTH EAST RESOURCE DEVELOPMENT COUNCIL
ISLAND LAKE TRIBAL COUNCIL

SASKATCHEWAN REGION   **TOTAL FUNDING PROVIDED:** $463,000

BANDS RECEIVING FUNDS:

AHTAHKAKOOP	KEY	PEEPEEKISIS
BEARDY'S AND OKEMASIS	KINISTINO	PELICAN LAKE
BIG C	LAC LA HACHE	PETER BALLANTYNE
BIG RIVER	LITTLE BLACK BEAR	PIAPOT
BLACK LAKE	LITTLE PINE	POUNDMAKER
BUFFALO RIVER	LUCKY MAN	RED EARTH
CANOE LAKE	MAKWA SAHGAIEHCAN	RED PHEASANT
CARRY THE KETTLE	MISTAWASIS	SAKIMAY
COTE	MONTREAL LAKE	SAULTEAUX
COWESSESS	MOOSE WOODS	SHOAL LAKE
CUMBERLAND HOUSE	MOOSOMIN	STANDING BUFFALO
FISHING LAKE	MUSKEG LAKE	STAR BLANKET
JAMES SMITH	NIKANEET	STURGEON LAKE
JOSEPH BIGHEAD	NUT LAKE	SWEET GRASS
JOHN SMITH	OCHAPOWACE	THUNDERCHILD
KAHKEWISTAHAW	OKANESE	WAHPETON
KEESEEKOOSE	ONION LAKE	WHITE BEAR
		WITCHEKAN LAKE

NATIVE ASSOCIATION RECEIVING FUNDING:

MEADOW LAKE DISTRICT CHIEF MANAGEMENT COMPANY LIMITED

APPENDIX C

BANDS AND ASSOCIATIONS IN RECEIPT OF FUNDING FOR THE DEVELOPMENT OF MEMBERSHIP RULES, MAY 31, 1987

ALBERTA REGION   **TOTAL FUNDING PROVIDED:** $266,500

BANDS RECEIVING FUNDS:

ALEXANDER	ERMINESKIN	PEIGAN
ALEXIS	FORT CHIPEWYAN	SADDLE LAKE
BEAVER LAKE	FORT McKAY	SARCEE
BIGSTONE CREE	FORT McMURRAY	STONEY (CHINIKI)
BLACKFOOT	HEART LAKE	STURGEON LAKE
BLOOD	HORSE LAKE	SUCKER CREEK
COLD LAKE FIRST NATIONS	JANVIER	SUNCHILD CREE
CREE	LITTLE RED RIVER	SWAN RIVER
DENE THA'	LUBICON LAKE	TALLCREE
DRIFTPILE	O'CHIESE	WHITEFISH LAKE
ENOCH	PAUL	

BRITISH COLUMBIA REGION   **TOTAL FUNDING PROVIDED:** $1,276,880

BANDS RECEIVING FUNDS:

ADAMS LAKE	KITAMAAT	PENELAKUT
ALEXANDRIA	KITKATLA	PENTICTON
ANAHAM	KITSEGUKLA	QUALICUM
ASHCROFT	KITSELAS	QUATSINO
BELLA COOLA	KITSUMKALUM	QUESNEL
BONAPARTE	KITWANCOOL	SAMAHQUAM
BOSTON BAR	KWAKIUTL	SAULTEAU
BURRARD	LAKALZAP	SCOWLITZ
CAMPBELL RIVER	LAX KW'ALAAMS	SETON LAKE
CANIM LAKE	LILLOOET	SKEETCHESTN
CANOE CREEK	LITTLE SHUSWAP LAKE	SKIDEGATE
CANYON CITY	LOWER SIMILKAMEEN	SKWAH
CAPE MUDGE	LYTTON	SODA CREEK
CHEMAINUS	MALAHAT	SONGHEES
COOK'S FERRY	MASSET	SPALLUMCHEEN
DOIG RIVER	McLEOD LAKE	SOUAMISH
GITANMAAX	METLAKATLA	STELLAQUO
GITLAKDAMIX	MORICETOWN	THALTAN
GLEN VOWELL	MUSQUEAM	TOBACCO PLAINS
HAGWILGET	NANAIMO	TSARTLIP
HARTLEY BAY	NANOOSE	TSAWOUT
HOMALCO	NAZKO	TSAWWASSEN
KAMLOOPS	NORTH THOMPSON	TSEYCUM
KATZIE	OHIAHT	UPPER SIMILKAMEEN
KINCOLITH	OSOYOOSAHT	WESTBANK
KISPIOX	PACHEENAHT	WHISPERING PINES
	PAUQUACHIN	WILLIAMS LAKE

APPENDIX C

BANDS AND ASSOCIATIONS IN RECEIPT OF FUNDING FOR THE DEVELOPMENT OF MEMBERSHIP RULES, MAY 31, 1987

NATIVE ASSOCIATION RECEIVING FUNDS:

CARRIER-SIKANI TRIBAL COUNCIL
DESOLUTION TRIBAL COUNCIL
KOOTENAY AREA COUNCIL
NICOLA VALLEY INDIAN ADMINISTRATION
NLAKA'PAMUX NATION TRIBAL COUNCIL
NUU-CHAH-NULTH TRIBAL COUNCIL
STO: LO NATION SOCIETY
TREATY 8 TRIBAL ASSOCIATION

YUKON REGION　　　　　　　　　　**TOTAL FUNDING PROVIDED:** $90,000

BANDS RECEIVING FUNDS:

CARCROSS-TAGISH	LITTLE SALMON-CARMACES
CHAMPAGNE	NA-CHO NY'A'K-DUN
DAWSON	OLD CROW
KLUANE	SELKIRK
KWANLIN DUN	TAKU RIVER TLINGIT
LIARD RIVER	TESLIN

NORTHWEST TERRITORIES REGION　　**TOTAL FUNDING PROVIDED:** $25,500

BANDS RECEIVING FUNDS:

FORT LIARD
FORT McPHERSON
INUVIK NATIVE

Other Native Associations not previously identified received an additional $45,500 for the development of membership rules.

APPENDIX D

BANDS PRESENTING MEMBERSHIP RULES

Bands in control of their membership as of
May 31, 1987:

REGION	NAME OF BAND	DATE RULES IN EFFECT
Ontario	Chippewas of Georgina Island	Feb. 27, 1987
	Wapekeka	July 15, 1987
Saskatchewan	Cumberland House	Sept. 16, 1985
Alberta	Driftpile	Nov. 9, 1986
	Ermineskin	July 2, 1986
	Fort McMurray	Jan. 2, 1987
	Horse Lake	June 3, 1986
	Lubicon Lake	Feb. 3, 1986
	Sawridge	July 8, 1985
	Swan River	Apr. 4, 1986
British Columbia	Saulteau	Nov. 17, 1986
	Sechelt	Sept. 19, 1985

Other bands that had forwarded membership rules to the
Minister as of May 31, 1987:

REGION	NAME OF BAND	DATE RECEIVED
Atlantic	Buctouche	*
	Miawpukek	*
Québec	Abenakis de Wolinak	May 1987
Ontario	Big Island	Apr. 1987
	McDowell Lake	Mar. 1987
	Moose Deer Point	May 1987
	North Spirit Lake	Mar. 1987
	Pays Plat	Apr. 1987
	Sandy Lake	Mar. 1987
	Whitesand	Dec. 1986

APPENDIX D (cont'd)

Manitoba	Buffalo Point	Mar. 1987
	Crane River	May 1987
	Lake St. Martin	Aug. 1986
Saskatchewan	Saulteaux	May 1987
Alberta	Alexander	May 1987
	Beaver Lake	*
	Enoch	May 1987
	Heart Lake	*
	Janvier	May 1987
	Kehewin	*
	Sucker Creek	May 1986
	Sunchild Cree	May 1987
	Tallcree	Apr. 1987
British Columbia	Alexandria	Apr. 1987
	Burrard	May 1987
	Canim Lake	Apr. 1987
	Glen Vowell	Apr. 1987
Yukon	Aishihik	Apr. 1987
	Champagne	Apr. 1987

Three bands had elected to leave control of their band list with the department as of May 31, 1987: Afton, Horton, Pictou Landing (all in the Atlantic region).

* Information was received, but it was returned to bands for clarification or change, with the option of their making a resubmission.

CANADA

L'honorable John A. Fraser, c.p., c.r., député,
Président de la Chambre des communes
OTTAWA (Ontario)
K1A 0A6

Monsieur le Président,

Conformément à l'article 22 de la <u>Loi modifiant la Loi
sur les Indiens</u> de 1985, c. 27, il me fait plaisir de
soumettre au Parlement ce rapport sur la mise en oeuvre
des modifications apportées à la <u>Loi sur les Indiens</u>.

Veuillez agréer, Monsieur le Président, mes salutations
les plus distinguées.

Bill McKnight

Rapport au Parlement

Mise en oeuvre des modifications apportées en 1985 à la Loi sur les Indiens

Affaires indiennes et du Nord Canada
Juin 1987

Affaires indiennes
et du Nord Canada
Indian and Northern
Affairs Canada

Publié avec l'autorisation de
l'hon. Bill McKnight, c.p., député,
ministre des Affaires indiennes
et du Nord canadien,
Ottawa, 1987.

QS-5234-000-BB-A1
N° de catalogue R32-83/1987
ISBN 0-662-55276-8

RÉSUMÉ

Deux ans se sont écoulés depuis que le Parlement a adopté le projet de loi C-31, modifiant la Loi sur les Indiens afin de l'harmoniser avec la Charte canadienne des droits et libertés.

L'adoption du projet de loi C-31 éliminait de la Loi sur les Indiens les dispositions discriminatoires fondées sur le sexe et abolissait le concept d'émancipation. Elle permettait également aux personnes qui avaient perdu leur statut d'Indien et leur appartenance à une bande à cause de ces dispositions discriminatoires, de recouvrer leurs droits, et à leurs enfants d'être reconnus comme Indiens inscrits. En outre, des dispositions du projet de loi C-31 habilitaient les bandes indiennes à fixer les règles d'appartenance à leur groupe, ouvrant ainsi la voie à l'instauration de l'autonomie gouvernementale.

Grâce à la collaboration d'associations autochtones, des particuliers dans tout le pays ont été informés des incidences du projet de loi C-31. Plusieurs d'entre eux ont demandé à être admis comme Indiens inscrits. Un certain nombre de bandes ont assumé le contrôle de leur effectif, et plusieurs autres sont en train d'élaborer leurs règles d'appartenance.

Seulement un petit nombre de particuliers sont retournés vivre dans les réserves au cours des deux premières années de la mise en oeuvre du projet de loi C-31, ce qui a eu peu de répercussions mesurables sur les terres et les ressources des bandes. Affaires indiennes et du Nord Canada continuera de suivre de près le nombre de personnes qui retournent vivre dans les réserves.

A cause des changements qui sont susceptibles de se produire durant les prochaines années, le Ministère entreprendra une évaluation précise des répercussions des modifications de 1985 et présentera un deuxième rapport en juin 1990.

RAPPORT AU PARLEMENT

MISE EN OEUVRE DES MODIFICATIONS APPORTÉES EN 1985

À LA LOI SUR LES INDIENS

TABLE DES MATIÈRES

LISTE DES FIGURES ET TABLEAUX

RAPPORT AU PARLEMENT
MISE EN OEUVRE DES MODIFICATIONS APPORTÉES EN 1985
À LA LOI SUR LES INDIENS

I. INTRODUCTION

Les modifications de la Loi sur les Indiens adoptées par le Parlement en juin 1985 revêtent une grande importance pour les Indiens du Canada. Elles marquent la fin de la discrimination fondée sur le sexe, apparue pour la première fois il y a cent ans dans un texte législatif touchant les Indiens. En outre, ces modifications rétablissent le statut d'Indien et le droit d'appartenance à une bande pour les personnes qui les ont perdus par le passé à cause des dispositions discriminatoires de la Loi. Leurs enfants ont également le droit de faire porter leur nom au Registre des Indiens. De plus, conformément à l'engagement pris par le gouvernement à l'égard de l'autonomie gouvernementale des Indiens, ces modifications permettent aux bandes indiennes d'assumer le contrôle de leur effectif.

Conformément à l'article 22 de la Loi modifiant la Loi sur les Indiens, à la suite des modifications apportées en 1985 par l'adoption du projet de loi C-31*, un rapport comprenant les renseignements suivants doit être présenté au Parlement :

o   le nombre de personnes inscrites en vertu de l'article 6 de la Loi sur les Indiens et le nombre de celles dont le nom a été porté à la liste de chaque bande aux termes du paragraphe 11(1) de la Loi, depuis le 17 avril 1985;

o   le nombre et les noms des bandes qui ont assumé le contrôle de leur effectif conformément à l'article 10 de la Loi sur les Indiens;

o   les répercussions des modifications sur les terres et sur les ressources des bandes indiennes.

On trouvera dans le chapitre II du rapport une description des activités entreprises pour appliquer ces modifications. Le chapitre III traite des demandes d'inscription et de rétablissement du droit d'appartenance à une bande.

---

*Statuts du Canada, 1985, chap. 27. Ce texte législatif est mentionné dans le présent rapport sous les désignations de "modifications de 1985 à la Loi sur les Indiens" ou de "projet de loi C-31".

Au chapitre IV, il est question de l'élaboration et de la mise en oeuvre des règles d'appartenance aux bandes. Au chapitre V, les répercussions des modifications sont étudiées à l'échelle locale et régionale, plus précisément en ce qui a trait aux dépenses liées aux programmes et aux services.

Les données relatives aux requérants du statut d'Indien ont été relevées le 31 mai 1987. Les données financières reflètent les dépenses encourues au 31 mars 1987.

II. ACTIVITÉS DE MISE EN OEUVRE

Pour mettre en oeuvre les modifications de 1985 à la Loi sur les Indiens, il a fallu s'assurer que les renseignements qui les concernent étaient diffusés à une grande échelle, répondre le plus tôt possible aux demandes et fournir des sommes additionnelles pour financer les programmes et les services. Ce chapitre traite des activités de communications et des changements survenus au Ministère pour permettre l'application de la Loi. Les fonds additionnels nécessaires au financement des programmes sont étudiés au chapitre V.

Communications

Les médias, Affaires indiennes et du Nord Canada et les associations indiennes ont tous joué un rôle important dans la diffusion de l'information concernant les modifications apportées à la Loi sur les Indiens. Une conférence de presse, donnée le jour où le projet de loi C-31 a été déposé à la Chambre des communes, a suscité de nombreux reportages à ce sujet, à l'échelle nationale. Les médias ont continué de couvrir l'événement tout au long du processus législatif, notamment en lui consacrant des articles de fond dans les grands quotidiens et en lui accordant du temps d'antenne au cours d'importantes émissions d'actualités comme The Journal. Les médias autochtones ont également couvert au jour le jour les délibérations du comité parlementaire sur le projet de loi et ont suivi régulièrement cette question pour leur public.

Après l'adoption des modifications, le ministère des Affaires indiennes et du Nord canadien a pris plusieurs mesures pour diffuser plus largement l'information sur les modifications de 1985. Le Ministère a conçu et mis en oeuvre un programme de communications publiques pour veiller à ce que les personnes intéressées soient au courant de cette initiative gouvernementale et informées de la marche à suivre pour obtenir le rétablissement de leur statut et de leur droit d'appartenance à une bande ou l'inscription pour la première fois.

On a produit des affiches et des trousses d'information pour transmettre ces renseignements. Plus de 160 000 exemplaires d'une brochure explicative ont été distribués, principalement aux collectivités autochtones, aux chefs et aux conseils de bande ainsi qu'aux associations autochtones. On a également fait parvenir du matériel d'information à d'autres parties intéressées, comme les députés et les sénateurs, les bibliothèques, les universités, les médias autochtones et le grand public.

Afin de pouvoir traiter directement les demandes précises relatives au rétablissement des droits, on a instauré un service téléphonique gratuit dès juin 1985. Ce numéro de libre appel (1-800-567-9605) continue de permettre un accès direct à des renseignements détaillés depuis n'importe quel endroit au Canada. En moyenne, une centaine d'appels y sont acheminés tous les jours.

Rôle des associations autochtones

Le gouvernement fédéral a reconnu le rôle important que pourraient jouer les associations autochtones en facilitant la mise en oeuvre des modifications. Après l'adoption de ces modifications, le gouvernement a invité les associations autochtones à proposer des projets visant à aider les particuliers à présenter une demande d'inscription. Depuis juin 1985, une subvention ponctuelle de 3,5 millions de dollars a été mise à la disposition de 18 associations. Ces subventions ont été accordées pour permettre aux associations autochtones d'informer les personnes les plus susceptibles d'être admissibles à l'inscription en vertu des dispositions de la Loi relatives au rétablissement du statut. On trouvera à l'annexe A une liste des bénéficiaires de subventions.

Changements survenus au Ministère

Le succès des efforts de communications et l'aide offerte aux particuliers par les associations autochtones peuvent se mesurer d'après le grand nombre de demandes d'inscription aux termes de la Loi sur les Indiens, dans sa version modifiée, reçues en date du 31 mai 1987. Le Ministère avait alors reçu 43 868 demandes d'inscription pour un nombre total de 90 051 personnes. La figure I indique le nombre de demandes reçues par mois depuis l'adoption des modifications.

Le nombre de demandes accueillies durant les deux premières années de la période de mise en oeuvre a suscité plusieurs changements au Ministère, dont le plus manifeste a été l'évolution de la Direction des droits et de l'effectif des bandes.

On prévoyait au départ que 31 années-personnes de plus seraient nécessaires au cours d'une période de 5 ans pour se charger des activités liées au rétablissement des droits. Cependant, étant donné le rythme plus rapide que prévu des demandes, et la somme de travail requise pour les recherches et l'étude de ces demandes, il est devenu évident qu'il fallait plus de personnel. En mai 1986, toutes les fonctions relatives à l'inscription des Indiens et à l'effectif des bandes ont été fusionnées en un seul service, et des années-personnes furent réaffectées au Ministère afin d'ajouter les ressources humaines nécessaires.

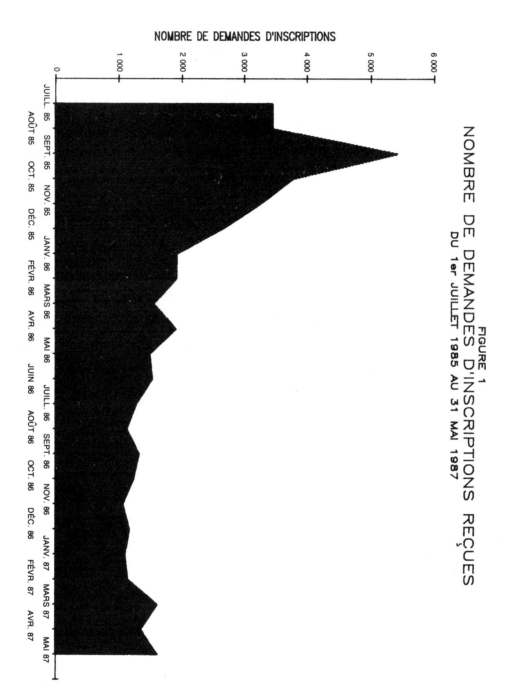

FIGURE 1
NOMBRE DE DEMANDES D'INSCRIPTIONS REÇUES
DU 1er JUILLET 1985 AU 31 MAI 1987

NOMBRE DE DEMANDES D'INSCRIPTIONS

III. PERSONNES DEMANDANT À RECEVOIR LE STATUT D'INDIEN

Par suite des modifications apportées en 1985 à la Loi sur les Indiens, toute personne qui a perdu son statut ou s'est vu refuser celui-ci, en raison des dispositions discriminatoires dans la loi antérieure, peut demander à être inscrite. La Loi sur les Indiens contient des dispositions relatives à l'existence d'un Registre des Indiens dirigé par un Registraire habilité à recevoir les demandes d'inscription, et dont le Ministère aurait la charge. Les personnes inscrites à ce registre sont reconnues comme détenant le statut d'Indien et, à ce titre, sont admissibles à certains avantages comme l'aide à l'éducation postsecondaire et des services de santé non assurés.

En vertu de la Loi sur les Indiens modifiée, les personnes qui ont le droit d'obtenir le statut d'Indien après en avoir fait la demande au Registraire sont les suivantes :

1. les femmes qui ont perdu leur statut en épousant un non-Indien;

2. les personnes qui ont perdu leur statut ou se sont vu refuser celui-ci en raison de toute autre disposition discriminatoire de la Loi sur les Indiens;

3. les personnes qui ont perdu leur statut pour cause d'émancipation; l'ancienne Loi contenait une disposition à l'effet qu'une personne pouvait échanger son statut d'Indien pour acquérir d'autres droits;

4. les enfants des personnes entrant dans l'une ou l'autre des catégories précédentes.

Comment déterminer l'admissibilité ?

C'est la Direction des droits et de l'effectif des bandes qui détermine si un particulier a le droit d'être inscrit en tant qu'Indien et s'il a le droit de se faire inscrire sur la liste de l'effectif d'une bande. Les intéressés sont invités à soumettre leur demande au Registraire, au ministère des Affaires indiennes et du Nord canadien, et leur droit d'inscription est évalué selon les critères définis à l'article 6 de la Loi sur les Indiens. La procédure comporte des recherches dans les dossiers du Ministère relativement à cette personne et à sa famille.

Ces dossiers comprennent le Registre des Indiens établi en vertu de la Loi sur les Indiens de 1951. Ce registre est classé par bande et contient les noms de toutes les personnes inscrites sur les listes de bande, ainsi que certaines données les concernant, comme les naissances, les décès et les mariages. Si l'on ne peut trouver l'information nécessaire dans le Registre, une recherche plus poussée et plus longue peut être effectuée dans les dossiers datant d'avant 1951, qui comprennent les traités et les listes de versement des annuités, les archives et les dossiers de recensement.

Les demandes d'inscription incomplètes rendent le processus plus difficile, par exemple, les demandes qui ne portent pas mention de la bande jusqu'à laquelle on pourrait retracer l'origine du requérant, ou qui ne contiennent pas d'informations sur les parents de ce dernier qui permettraient de confirmer son droit au statut d'Indien. Il faut alors demander au requérant de fournir des renseignements ou des documents supplémentaires, tels que des certificats de naissance ou de mariage. Tout cela entraîne souvent de longs retards avant qu'une décision puisse être prise sur les droits du requérant.

Nombre de personnes demandant à être inscrites

Au 31 mai 1987, la Direction des droits et de l'effectif des bandes avait reçu des demandes d'inscription touchant 90 051 personnes. La figure 2 fait état des nouvelles demandes d'inscription reçues par région, comparées au nombre d'Indiens inscrits en 1985.

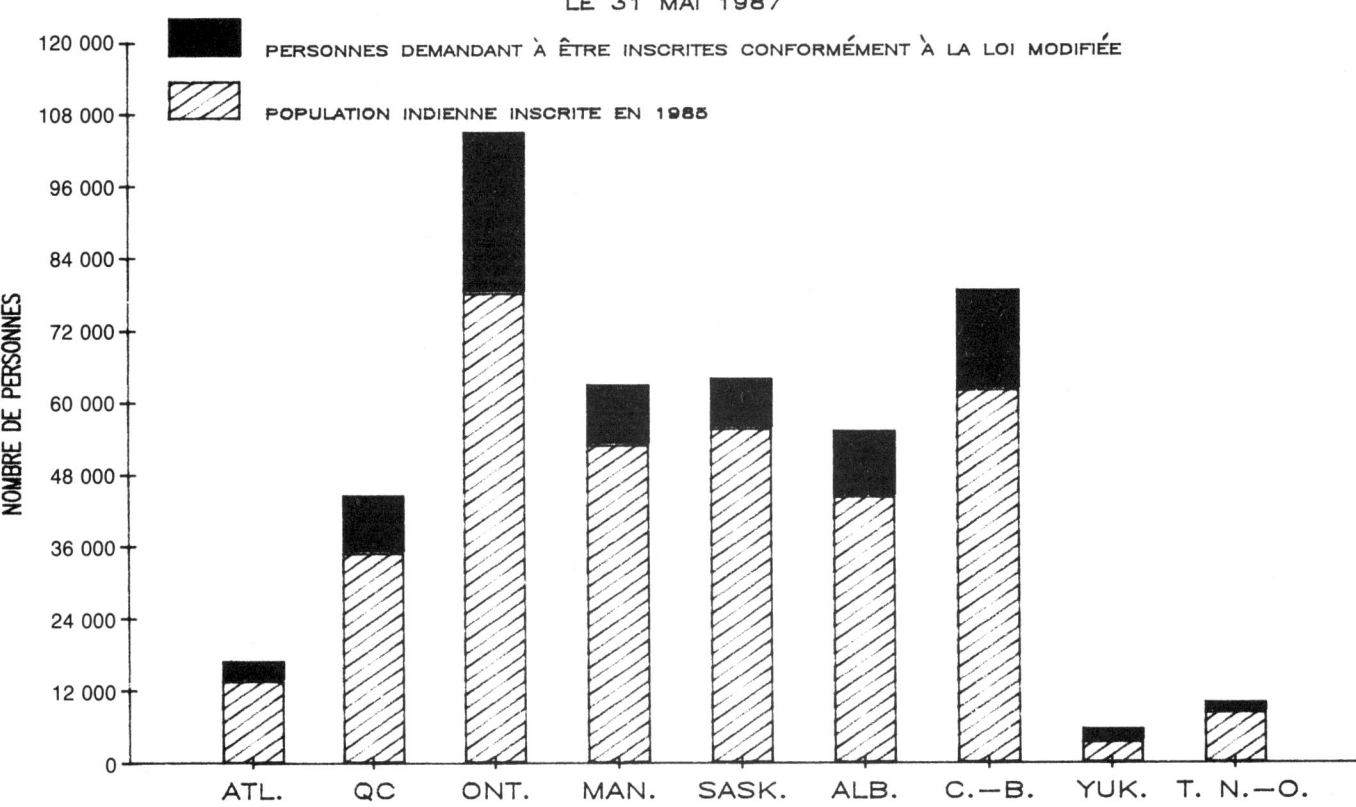

FIGURE 2
NOMBRE DE REQUÉRANTS PAR RÉGION
LE 31 MAI 1987

POPULATION INDIENNE INSCRITE = 355 321: REQUÉRANTS = 90 051

A cette date, les demandes de 63 p. 100 des 90 051 requérants avaient été étudiées. Une décision finale avait été rendue dans le cas de 34 p. 100 de tous les requérants. Les demandes de 29 p. 100 des requérants avaient été prises en considération et il faudra obtenir d'eux des informations supplémentaires, ou faire effectuer des recherches généalogiques avant qu'une décision finale ne soit prise. La figure 3 illustre l'état actuel des demandes d'inscription. Les demandes au sujet desquelles il faut obtenir des informations supplémentaires et effectuer des recherches plus poussées sont classées dans la catégorie "en cours".

FIGURE 3
ÉTAT DES DEMANDES D'INSCRIPTION AU REGISTRE DES INDIENS
LE 31 MAI 1987

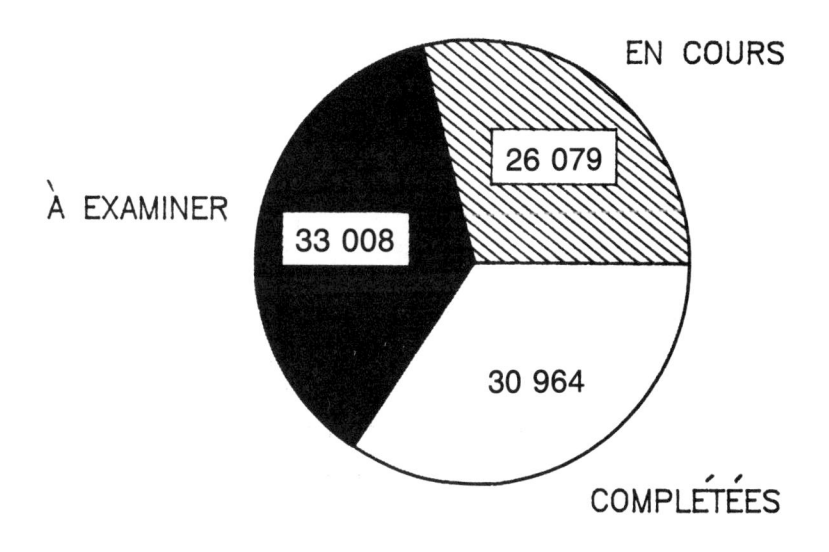

NOMBRE TOTAL DE REQUÉRANTS = 90 051

La figure 4 ci-dessous indique la répartition régionale des 24 708 personnes qui ont été déterminées admissibles à l'inscription en vertu des modifications apportées à la Loi sur les Indiens, et cela au 31 mai 1987.

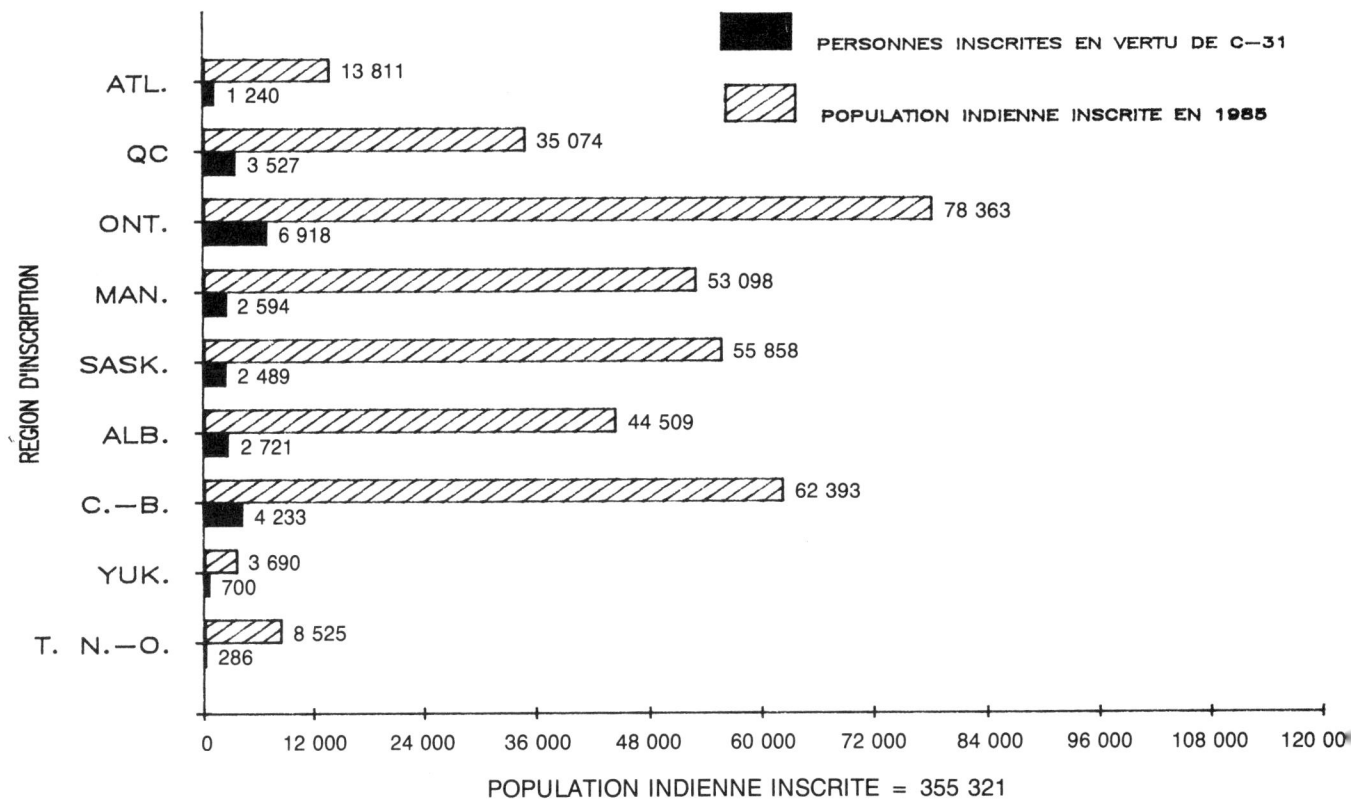

FIGURE, 4
INSCRIPTIONS COMPLÉTÉES PAR RÉGION
LE 31 MAI 1987

POPULATION INDIENNE INSCRITE = 355 321

PERSONNES INSCRITES EN VERTU DE L'ARTICLE 6 : 24 708

Parmi les personnes restantes dont les demandes avaient été traitées avant le 31 mai 1987, on en comptait 1 769 dont le nom avait déjà été inscrit dans le Registre des Indiens. On avait débouté de leur demande 2 939 autres personnes. De plus, les noms de 1 425 autres personnes figuraient sur plus d'une demande officielle. Les 123 personnes restantes avaient adressé des demandes à la Direction des droits et de l'effectif des bandes mais sans rapport avec l'inscription aux termes des nouvelles dispositions de la Loi; leurs demandes ont été dirigées au service pertinent du Ministère.

Admissibilité aux bandes

Au 31 mai 1987, 36 p. 100 des 24 708 personnes qui étaient inscrites en vertu de l'article 6 avaient le droit de recouvrer immédiatement leur statut de membre d'une bande conformément au paragraphe 11(1) de la Loi sur les Indiens. Le nombre total de ces personnes est ventilé par Région à la figure 5.

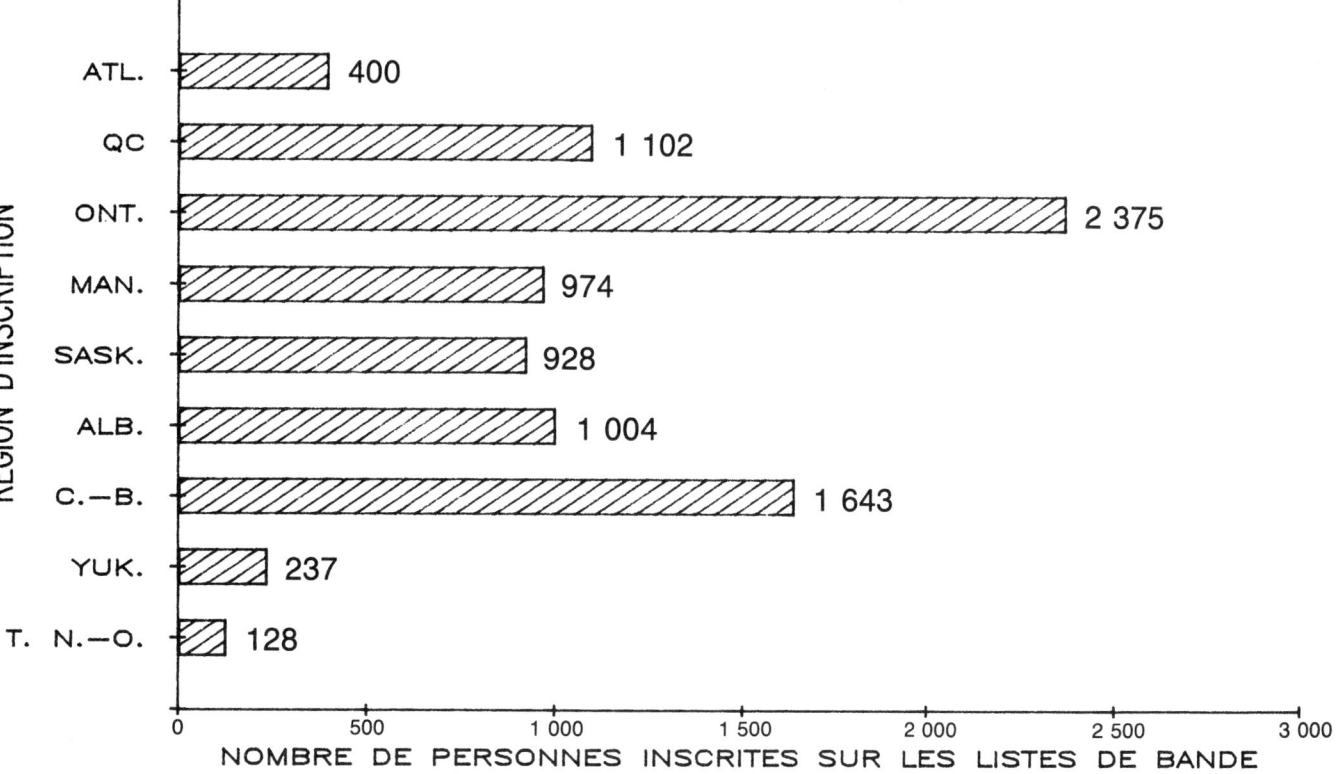

FIGURE 5
PERSONNES INSCRITES SUR LES LISTES DE BANDE
LE 31 MAI 1987

PERSONNES INSCRITES SUR LISTES DE BANDE EN VERTU DU PARAGRAPHE 11(1)=8 791

Dans le cas des autres personnes qui demandent le statut d'Indien, l'appartenance à une bande est assujettie aux dispositions de l'article 10 ou du paragraphe 11(2) de la Loi sur les Indiens. Pendant la période de deux ans qui prend fin le 28 juin 1987, les bandes peuvent élaborer des règles d'appartenance établissant leurs propres critères d'admissibilité. Si une bande ne prend pas les mesures nécessaires pour assumer le contrôle de son effectif durant ces deux ans, les dispositions de la Loi sur les Indiens s'appliqueront et la plupart des Indiens inscrits auront le droit d'appartenir à une bande.

Statistiques pour chaque bande

On trouvera à l'annexe B des statistiques relatives aux bandes, notamment le nombre de personnes qui demandent à être inscrites, le nombre d'inscriptions et le nombre de personnes inscrites sur les listes de bande, pour chacune des bandes.

IV. ÉLABORATION DES RÈGLES D'APPARTENANCE AUX BANDES

Le droit de déterminer l'appartenance aux bandes est un des aspects importants de l'autonomie gouvernementale, et les modifications apportées en 1985 à la Loi sur les Indiens donnent aux bandes le moyen d'agir en ce sens. L'article 10 de la Loi sur les Indiens définit la façon dont les bandes peuvent assumer le contrôle de leur propre effectif. Ainsi, la majorité des électeurs doit voter en faveur du contrôle de l'effectif par la bande et en faveur des règles élaborées par la bande pour que ces mesures soient valides. D'autres dispositions voient à protéger les droits acquis des membres de la bande et les droits de ceux qui sont admissibles à recouvrer leur statut de membre de la bande.

La Loi sur les Indiens modifiée offre aux bandes la possibilité d'assumer le contrôle de leur effectif quand elles le désirent. Si une bande ne prend pas de mesures pour assumer le contrôle de son effectif pendant la période de deux ans se terminant le 28 juin 1987, la reconnaissance, par le gouvernement fédéral, du statut d'Indien d'une personne sera en principe suffisant pour conférer à cette personne le statut de membre de la bande. Les personnes qui deviendront membre d'une bande de cette façon acquerront alors des droits qui devront être respectés dans toutes les règles d'appartenance qu'une bande pourrait éventuellement adopter.

Financement des initiatives des bandes

Une somme totale de 6,5 millions de dollars a été mise de côté par le gouvernement fédéral pour aider les bandes à élaborer et à mettre en oeuvre leurs règles d'appartenance. Au 31 mai 1987, 490 bandes avaient demandé et reçu des subventions à cette fin (voir figure 6). Les fonds distribués à ces bandes s'élèvent à 3,6 millions de dollars. De plus, cinq bandes avaient reçu des subventions d'un montant total de 46 500 $ afin de mettre en oeuvre leurs règles d'appartenance et de tenir des listes de membres. On trouvera à l'annexe C une liste des bandes qui ont reçu des fonds pour élaborer des règles d'appartenance.

Les bandes font parvenir au Ministre les règles d'appartenance qu'elles ont élaborées, accompagnées d'un document faisant état de l'approbation de l'électorat. On examine ces règles pour déterminer si elles répondent aux exigences de l'article de la Loi sur les Indiens modifiée qui touche la protection des droits acquis. On étudie également la documentation justificative établissant que la majorité des électeurs a voté en faveur du transfert du contrôle et en faveur des règles d'appartenance. Si ces conditions sont satisfaites, le Ministre informe la bande que le contrôle de son effectif lui est transféré. Si, au contraire,

les nouvelles règles ne répondent pas aux exigences susmentionnées, elles sont retournées à la bande pour que celle-ci reprenne le dossier.

FIGURE 6
BANDES AYANT REÇU DES FONDS
POUR L'ÉLABORATION DE RÈGLES D'APPARTENANCE
LE 31 MAI 1987

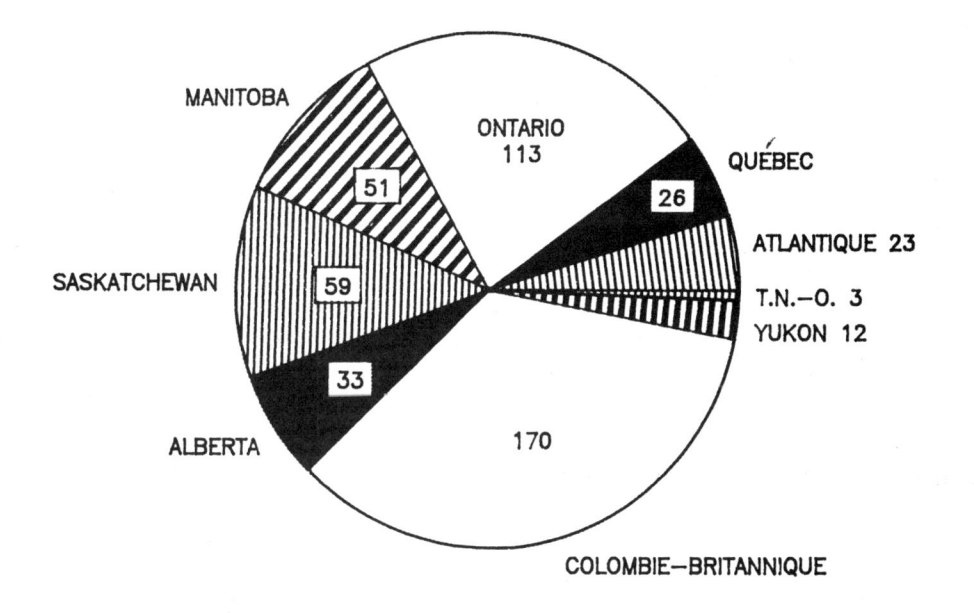

NOMBRE TOTAL DES BANDES AYANT REÇU DES FONDS = 490

Élaboration des règles d'appartenance

Au 31 mai 1987, le Ministre avait transféré à 20 bandes le contrôle de leur effectif (voir tableau 1). Vingt-neuf autres bandes ont envoyé la documentation pertinente (annexe D) et leurs demandes sont en cours d'examen. Trois bandes ont choisi de laisser ce contrôle au Ministère. On peut s'attendre qu'une bonne partie des autres bandes qui ont reçu des fonds pour élaborer leurs règles d'appartenance demandent que ces règles soient reconnues.

Tableau 1

BANDES EXERÇANT LE CONTRÔLE DE LEUR EFFECTIF

Le 31 mai 1987

Bande	Règles en vigueur
Sawridge (Alberta)	Le 8 juillet 1985
Cumberland House (Saskatchewan)	Le 16 septembre 1985
Sechelt (Colombie-Britannique)	Le 19 septembre 1985
Lubicon Lake (Alberta)	Le 3 février 1986
Swan River (Alberta)	Le 4 avril 1986
Horse Lake (Alberta)	Le 3 juin 1986
Ermineskin (Alberta)	Le 2 juillet 1986
Wapekeka (Ontario)	Le 15 juillet 1986
Driftpile (Alberta)	Le 9 novembre 1986
Saulteau (Colombie-Britannique)	Le 17 novembre 1986
Fort McMurray (Alberta)	Le 2 janvier 1987
Chippewas de Georgina Island (Ontario)	Le 27 février 1987

V. RÉPERCUSSIONS SUR LES TERRES ET LES RESSOURCES

Les modifications apportées en 1985 à la Loi sur les Indiens ont des répercussions qui sont ressenties de plusieurs façons. Les personnes qui ont obtenu le statut d'Indien et qui sont désireuses de s'installer dans les réserves peuvent avoir un impact sur la prestation des programmes et des services dans ces réserves. Pour mesurer ces répercussions possibles, le Ministère a examiné les demandes des bandes pour obtenir des fonds supplémentaires destinés à financer les programmes et services auxquels les nouveaux résidants ont droit. Une autre source de renseignements sur les répercussions des modifications se trouve dans les demandes individuelles de services de la part d'Indiens nouvellement inscrits qui vivent à l'extérieur des réserves, ou venant d'Indiens dont la bande ne fournit pas les services dont ils ont besoin.

Ce chapitre contient de l'information quant au nombre connu des personnes qui veulent retourner vivre dans les réserves ainsi qu'à l'augmentation des dépenses liées aux programmes et aux services. À ce jour, seul un petit nombre de personnes sont retournées dans les réserves. Par conséquent, on ne connaît pas encore l'étendue des répercussions des modifications. Le Ministère est donc obligé de continuer à surveiller les répercussions de la mise en oeuvre du projet de loi C-31.

Personnes désirant retourner vivre dans les réserves

Au 31 mai 1987, les demandes formulées par les bandes en vue d'obtenir des fonds supplémentaires pour les programmes et les services destinés aux personnes nouvellement inscrites indiquaient que 1 424 personnes avaient l'intention de retourner dans les réserves d'ici 1 990. Cela pourrait causer une augmentation inférieure à 1 p. 100 de la population totale des réserves indiennes. Le tableau 2 fait état de la répartition régionale des personnes qui, selon les bandes, veulent retourner dans les réserves.

Tableau 2

PERSONNES NOUVELLEMENT INSCRITES ET DÉSIREUSES DE RETOURNER DANS LES RÉSERVES

Région	Population des réserves en juin 1985	Nombre de personnes inscrites désireuses de retourner dans les réserves (chiffres fournis par les bandes Le 31 mai 1987	Nombre de bandes demandant des fonds pour les personnes désireuses de retourner dans les réserves Le 31 mai 1987
Atlantique	9 985	82	6
Québec	29 987	193	7
Ontario	53 312	158	13
Manitoba	39 175	290	13
Saskatchewan	36 895	41	8
Alberta	33 532	2	0
Colombie-Britannique	39 860	469	45
Yukon	2 772	189	11
T. N.-O.	7 981	0	0
Canada	253 499	1 424	103

Coûts supplémentaires des programmes

Les personnes qui acquièrent le statut d'Indien à la suite des modifications apportées en 1985 à la Loi sur les Indiens ont droit aux programmes et services fédéraux au même titre que les autres personnes dont le nom figure sur le Registre des Indiens. Qu'ils vivent à l'intérieur ou à l'extérieur des réserves, les Indiens inscrits peuvent demander une aide à l'éducation postsecondaire par l'intermédiaire d'Affaires indiennes et du Nord Canada, ainsi que des services de santé non assurés fournis par Santé et Bien-être social Canada.

De plus, le gouvernement fédéral fournit des programmes et des services aux Indiens vivant dans les réserves qui s'apparentent beaucoup à ceux que les gouvernements provinciaux et municipaux fournissent aux autres particuliers. Dans le cas des personnes qui vivent dans les réserves, le gouvernement fédéral fournit des fonds pour le logement, l'éducation primaire et secondaire, les services de santé et l'aide sociale, services qui sont pour la plupart dispensés par les bandes et les conseils tribaux.

Affaires indiennes et du Nord Canada supporte le coût supplémentaire de la prestation des services et programmes des personnes qui ont recouvré leur statut d'Indien à la suite des modifications de 1985, que ces services et programmes soient fournis directement par le Ministère, ou, plus souvent, par une bande ou un conseil tribal. L'admissibilité et les autres critères liés à ces programmes s'appliquent aux personnes qui viennent d'acquérir le statut d'Indien aussi bien qu'à tous les autres Indiens dont le nom est inscrit au Registre des Indiens.

Dépenses liées aux programmes et aux services : Affaires indiennes et du Nord Canada

Du 1er juillet 1985 au 31 mars 1987, Affaires indiennes et du Nord Canada a dépensé 29 millions de dollars spécialement pour financer la mise en oeuvre du projet de loi C-31 et pour fournir des services aux personnes nouvellement inscrites à la suite de l'adoption de ce projet de loi. On a dépensé 4 millions de dollars au cours de l'année financière 1985-1986, et 25 millions de dollars en 1986-1987.

Le tableau 3 fait état, pour chaque année financière, des dépenses d'Affaires indiennes et du Nord Canada qui sont directement liées aux modifications apportées à la Loi sur les Indiens en 1985. La plus grande partie de ces fonds a été consacrée à l'aide à l'éducation postsecondaire, au logement et aux communications relatives au projet de loi C-31, ainsi qu'à l'élaboration des règles d'appartenance aux bandes. Ce tableau montre les fonds accordés à divers organismes autochtones pour soutenir leurs efforts en vue d'informer et d'aider les particuliers qui ont le droit d'être inscrits aux termes de la Loi sur les Indiens modifiée et le financement fourni aux bandes pour élaborer et appliquer leurs règles d'appartenance. Le tableau 3 fait également état des dépenses prévues par le projet de loi C-31 à l'égard des immobilisations communautaires. Ces fonds supplémentaires ont surtout été utilisés pour financer la construction de réseaux d'adduction d'eau, d'évacuation des eaux usées, de routes, et des autres infrastructures nécessaires à la construction de logements.

En général, le financement des programmes destinés aux bandes est approuvé par les bureaux régionaux du Ministère, et les fonds sont alors transférés aux bandes dans le cadre d'accords de contributions. Cette approche communautaire permet de faire en sorte que les fonds soient distribués conformément à la situation des collectivités. D'autre part, afin de rendre compte de l'utilisation des fonds selon les exigences du gouvernement fédéral, le Ministère doit recevoir de la part des bandes, des conseils tribaux et des particuliers qui ont reçu des

contributions, les renseignements voulus pour procéder à une double vérification. Premièrement, les personnes qui bénéficient des services doivent être inscrites. Deuxièmement, les montants demandés doivent être raisonnables.

Au tableau 4, on peut voir le lien existant entre les dépenses liées aux programmes et aux services résultant des modifications de 1985 et les dépenses totales liées aux programmes et services fournis aux Indiens par le ministère des Affaires indiennes et du Nord canadien. Les programmes et services pris en considération sont les terres, les revenus et les fiducies; l'éducation primaire et secondaire; l'éducation postsecondaire; l'aide sociale; les services de bien-être; les autres services éducatifs et sociaux; le développement économique; la gestion des bandes; les immobilisations; le logement; le maintien de l'ordre et l'administration.

L'aide financière accordée pour l'éducation postsecondaire aux 1 730 personnes nouvellement inscrites en vertu du projet de loi C-31 représente 6 p. 100 des dépenses totales du Ministère destinées à l'éducation postsecondaire effectuées du 1er juillet 1985 au 31 mars 1987. Les subventions de logement accordées à la suite des modifications et qui touchent 347 logements constituent 5 p. 100 des dépenses totales de logement effectuées par le Ministère pendant la même période. Si l'on excepte le financement unique destiné aux activités de communications ainsi qu'à l'élaboration et à la mise en oeuvre des règles d'appartenance, les dépenses liées aux programmes découlant de l'application des modifications représentent moins de 1 p. 100 du total des dépenses effectuées par le Programme des affaires indiennes et inuit du 1er juillet 1985 au 31 mars 1987.

TABLEAU 3

DÉPENSES POUR LES PROGRAMMES ET LES SERVICES RELIÉS AU PROJET DE LOI C-31

Destination des fonds	Dépenses du 1er juillet 1985 au 31 mars 1986 (en milliers de dollars)	Dépenses du 1er avril 1986 au 31 mars 1987 (en milliers de dollars)	Total des dépenses du 1er juillet 1985 au 31 mars 1987 (en milliers de dollars)
Communications et règles d'appartenance	3 005	4 056	7 061
Éducation primaire et secondaire	0	351	351
Éducation postsecondaire	929	8 248	9 176
Aide sociale	0	370	370
Services de bien-être	0	11	11
Autres services éducatifs et sociaux	0	11	11
Développement économique	37	944	981
Gestion des bandes	0	17	17
Immobilisations communautaires	0	2 360	2 360
Logement	0	8 619	8 619
Administration	81	10	91
TOTAL	4 052	24 996	29 047

TABLEAU 4

DÉPENSES POUR LE PROJET DE LOI C-31 ET LE PROGRAMME DES AFFAIRES INDIENNES ET INUIT (PAII)

Destination des fonds	PAII dépenses du 1er juillet 1985 au 31 mars 1987 (en milliers de dollars)	Dépenses liées au projet de loi C-31 du 1er juillet 1985 au 31 mars 1987 (en milliers de dollars)	Dépenses liées au projet de loi C-31 en pourcentage des dépenses totales du PAII du 1er juillet 1985 au 31 mars 1987 (en %)
Terres, revenus et fiducie	61 996	7 061 *	11,39
Éducation primaire et secondaire	704 946	351	0,05
Éducation postsecondaire	156 048	9 176	5,88
Aide sociale	464 477	370	0,08
Services de bien-être	155 043	11	0,01
Autres services éducatifs et sociaux	22 426	11	0,05
Développement économique	160 363	17	0,01
Gestion des bandes	224 408	981	0,44
Immobilisations communautaires	577 932	2 360	0,41
Logement	182 039	8 619	4,73
Maintien de l'ordre	29 021	0	0,00
Administration	143 246	91	0,06
TOTAL	2 881 944	29 047	1,01

* Pour ce qui est du projet de loi C-31, cette catégorie consiste presque exclusivement en un financement unique destiné aux activités de communications ainsi qu'à l'élaboration et à la mise en oeuvre des règles d'appartenance.

Financement des litiges

Au 31 mars 1987, un montant de 41 000 $ avait été fourni pour deux causes reliées au projet de loi C-31. L'une de ces causes porte sur la question de savoir si la décision d'ajouter le nom d'un particulier à une liste de bande, prise par le Registraire du Ministère avant le 17 avril 1985, peut être annulée par une protestation des membres de la bande touchée. La seconde a trait à une question constitutionnelle soulevée par six bandes de l'Alberta qui contestent certains articles de la Loi sur les Indiens modifiée. Dans ce dernier cas, des fonds ont été fournis au Conseil national des Autochtones du Canada (Alberta) et au Comité national pour la défense des droits des Indiennes.

Dépenses des programmes et des services : Santé et Bien-être social Canada

Santé et Bien-être social Canada accorde des fonds pour le financement des services de santé non assurés pour tous les Indiens inscrits. Ces services touchent les transports, les médicaments, les soins dentaires, les lunettes, les prestations de soins de santé et les services de santé donnés à contrat. En outre, Santé et Bien-être social Canada assure l'accès aux traitements ainsi qu'aux activités de prévention de la maladie et de promotion de la santé aux Indiens vivant dans les réserves.

Santé et Bien-être social Canada estime que les dépenses per capita pour tous les Indiens inscrits se sont élevées à 395,80 $ en 1985-1986, et à 443,40 $ en 1986-1987. Les dépenses liées aux personnes nouvellement inscrites en vertu du projet de loi C-31 ne sont pas calculées séparément. L'application des estimations per capita aux personnes nouvellement inscrites fait passer le total de l'estimation des dépenses à 2,5 millions de dollars en 1985-1986, et à 9,2 millions de dollars en 1986-1987. Si l'on excepte les dépenses pour services de santé non assurés, aucune dépense supplémentaire n'aura été engagée pour la prestation des services de santé aux Indiens inscrits à la suite des modifications de 1985 à la Loi sur les Indiens.

Indicateurs mesurables des répercussions futures

Au cours des prochaines années, on peut s'attendre que davantage de personnes nouvellement inscrites retourneront dans les réserves. C'est pourquoi il est important de continuer à évaluer les répercussions que pourraient avoir les modifications de 1985. Les secteurs qui pourraient être touchés sont l'éducation, le logement, l'emploi, le développement économique, la santé, l'aide sociale et la disponibilité des terres et des ressources (ainsi que leur gestion).

Les indicateurs relatifs à l'enseignement dispensé dans les réserves seront les changements au chapitre de l'inscription scolaire. Les répercussions relatives au logement seront évaluées en fonction du nombre de demandes de logements et de l'infrastructure nécessaires aux nouveaux résidants. Les indicateurs relatifs à l'emploi et au développement économique sont les changements qui se produisent dans les taux d'emploi, dans l'accessibilité à la formation, et dans la demande des programmes de prêts. On sera également attentif aux changements qui se produiront dans les besoins en matière de santé et d'aide sociale.

Il est encore trop tôt pour savoir quelles seront toutes les répercussions sur les terres des réserves et les ressources des bandes des modifications apportées en 1985 à la Loi sur les Indiens. Des changements pouvant se produire au cours des prochaines années, le ministère évaluera les répercussions des modifications de 1985 sur le secteur des terres et des ressources et présentera un rapport en juin 1990. Dans le cadre de cette évaluation, on fera rapport de l'expérience actuelle du retour dans les réserves des personnes nouvellement inscrites à la suite des modifications de la Loi.

VI. CONCLUSION

Les trois principes qui ont présidé à la formulation des modifications apportées en 1985 à la Loi sur les Indiens étaient les suivantes : la suppression de la discrimination, le recouvrement du statut d'Indien et du droit d'appartenance à une bande, et l'augmentation des pouvoirs exercés par les bandes indiennes sur leurs propres affaires. Avec l'adoption du projet de loi C-31, les clauses discriminatoires de la Loi sur les Indiens ont été supprimées. Pour ce qui est du recouvrement du statut et du contrôle exercé par les bandes sur leur effectif, les changements nécessaires ne se feront pas du jour au lendemain. Des progrès importants ont toutefois été réalisés au cours des deux premières années suivant l'adoption des modifications.

Le fait que près de 90 051 personnes se sont présentées pour demander que leur identité d'Indien soit reconnue par le gouvernement fédéral indique que les programmes de communications et d'information sont une réussite. En outre, plus des quatre cinquièmes de toutes les bandes au Canada sont en train d'élaborer leurs propres règles d'appartenance, et cela à des degrés divers. Le gouvernement fédéral a fourni des fonds pour supporter l'augmentation des coûts de la prestation des programmes à la suite des modifications de la Loi, et ces fonds ont été mis à la disposition des bandes, des conseils tribaux et des particuliers.

Affaires indiennes et du Nord Canada relève le défi administratif que constitue le traitement du nombre important de demandes d'inscription déjà reçues. Le Ministère continuera d'étudier les répercussions qu'auront les modifications sur le secteur des terres et des ressources ainsi que sur la prestation des services et autres avantages aux personnes nouvellement inscrites.

ANNEXE A

BÉNÉFICIAIRES DU FINANCEMENT DESTINÉ AUX ACTIVITÉS DE COMMUNICATIONS

Association	Montant
Alliance autochtone du Québec	134 148 $
Assemblée des premières nations	322 528 $
Association des femmes autochtones du Canada	1 062 370 $
Association des femmes autochtones du Québec	138 575 $
Association des Métis et des Indiens non inscrits du Nouveau-Brunswick	95 220 $
Association des Métis et des Indiens non inscrits de l'Ontario	287 500 $
Association des Métis des Territoires du Nord-Ouest	186 875 $
Association des Métis et des Indiens non inscrits de la Saskatchewan	100 050 $
Comité national pour la défense des droits des Indiennes	68 770 $
Conseil des Autochtones de l'Ile-du-Prince-Édouard	43 125 $
Conseil des Autochtones du Manitoba	150 420 $
Conseil des Autochtones de la Nouvelle-Écosse	70 150 $
Conseil des Indiens du Yukon	107 640 $
Conseil national des Autochtones du Canada	257 428 $
Conseil national des Autochtones du Canada - Alberta	121 670 $
Indian Homemakers Association of B.C.	107 916 $
United Native Nations (B.C.)	216 315 $
Winnipeg Council of Treaty and Status Indians	29 300 $
Total	3 500 000 $

ANNEXE B

STATISTIQUES POUR CHAQUE BANDE

Introduction

La présente annexe contient des informations sur le nombre de personnes qui demandent à être inscrites en vertu de la Loi sur les Indiens modifiée ainsi que sur le nombre total de personnes qui ont été inscrites et sur le nombre de celles dont le nom a été ajouté à des listes de bande conformément au paragraphe 11(1) du projet de loi C-31 adopté, au 31 mai 1987.

Le terme "bande inconnue" est utilisé dans la liste des bandes et renvoie aux personnes qui ont demandé leur inscription à la Direction des droits et de l'effectif des bandes sans indiquer la bande dont ils veulent faire partie, ou en l'indiquant incorrectement.

Les chiffres utilisés tout au long du rapport relativement à la population indienne inscrite sont ceux qui étaient en vigueur lorsque le projet de loi C-31 a été adopté. Il est donc impossible que les personnes inscrites après l'adoption du projet de loi C-31 soient comptées deux fois : une fois comme personne nouvellement inscrite, et une fois comme membre de la population de base.

Les Six-Nations de Grand River se composent des treize bandes suivantes, qui sont énumérées séparément dans la présente annexe :

Mohawks de la baie de Quinte
Bearfoot Onondaga
Deleware
Konodaha Seneca
Lower Cayuga
Lower Mohawk
Niharon Dasa Seneca

Oneida
Onondaga Clear Sky
Tuscarora
Upper Cayuga
Upper Mohawk
Walker Mohawk

Lorsqu'une personne demande à faire partie des Six-Nations de Grand River sans préciser dans quelle bande, elle est inscrite au titre de Six-Nations de Grand River. Dès que la bande a été précisée, le nom de cette personne est inscrit dans la liste appropriée.

NOM DE LA BANDE	NOMBRE TOTAL DE DEMANDES D'INSCRIPTION AU 87-05-31	NOMBRE TOTAL DES INSCRIPTIONS AU 87-05-31	NOMBRE TOTAL DE PERSONNES INSCRITES SUR LES LISTES DES BANDES AU 87-05-31	POPULATION INDIENNE INSCRITE JUIN 1985	POPULATION DES RÉSERVES JUIN 1985
ATLANTIQUE					
ABEGWEIT	39	9	5	221	159
ACADIA	227	67	21	386	73
AFTON	56	24	2	253	171
BEAR RIVER	79	17	8	110	41
BIG COVE	166	58	19	1502	1407
BUCTOUCHE	9	2	0	46	15
BURNT CHURCH	108	49	16	835	709
CHAPEL ISLAND	51	19	8	263	220
EDMUNDSTON	101	30	11	87	71
EEL GROUND	149	57	15	458	308
EEL RIVER	64	14	7	311	209
ESKASONI	110	47	14	1994	1839
FORT FOLLY	9	0	0	47	28
HORTON	46	17	9	82	11
INDIAN ISLAND	23	1	0	79	47
KINGSCLEAR	99	35	14	440	303
LENNOX ISLAND	218	41	14	381	227
MEMBERTOU	115	64	13	500	390
MIAWPUKEK	2	0	0	622	0
MILLBROOK	181	76	16	459	284
OROMOCTO	195	38	14	178	131
PABINEAU	85	30	14	67	51
PICTOU LANDING	47	17	7	318	232
RED BANK	53	26	13	302	263
SAINT MARY'S	212	78	37	548	396
SHUBENACADIE	139	32	13	1100	731
TOBIQUE	394	268	71	894	658
VALLÉE D'ANNAPOLIS	52	18	8	107	60
WAGMATCOOK	32	20	5	392	334
WHYCOCOMAGH	12	8	2	482	450
WOODSTOCK	192	78	24	347	167
ATLANTIQUE - BANDES INCONNUES	75	0	0	0	0
TOTAL POUR L'ATLANTIQUE	3340	1240	400	13811	9985
QUÉBEC					
ABÉNAKIS DE WOLINAK	143	41	7	83	52
ABITIBIWINNI	69	15	9	485	349
BETSIAMITES	124	46	15	2161	2044
CHISASIBI	133	20	9	1901	1835

NOM DE LA BANDE	NOMBRE TOTAL DE DEMANDES D'INSCRIPTION AU 87-05-31	NOMBRE TOTAL DES INSCRIPTIONS AU 87-05-31	NOMBRE TOTAL DE PERSONNES INSCRITES SUR LES LISTES DES BANDES AU 87-05-31	POPULATION INDIENNE INSCRITE JUIN 1985	POPULATION DES RÉSERVES JUIN 1985
EASTMAIN	3	0	0	368	321
GASPE	237	71	17	173	1
GRAND LAC VICTORIA	25	1	1	266	263
GRANDE RIVIÈRE DE LA BALEINE	4	4	2	417	402
KAHNAWAKE	1051	401	159	5450	5360
KANESATAKE	641	265	74	958	695
KIPAWA	207	64	20	202	139
LAC BARRIÈRE	60	32	8	399	348
LAC SIMON	103	12	7	590	473
LONGUE POINTE	100	29	9	355	237
MANOUANE	26	4	2	1166	1121
MICMACS DE MARIA	234	70	14	554	386
MINGAN	0	0	0	344	334
MISTASSINI	156	80	21	2244	1935
MONTAGNAIS DE NATASHQUAN	21	17	6	469	459
MONTAGNAIS DE SCHEFFERVILLE	42	9	2	493	487
MONTAGNAIS DE SEPT-ÎLES ET MALIOTENAM	463	144	50	1746	1643
MONTAGNAIS DES ESCOUMINS	250	73	26	144	114
MONTAGNAIS DU LAC SAINT-JEAN	1303	514	135	2023	1489
NASKAPIS DE SCHEFFERVILLE	9	1	0	396	378
NATION HURONNE WENDAT	1306	637	200	1292	775
NEMASKA	8	2	1	232	229
OBEDJIWAN	16	12	2	1237	1090
ODANAK	451	227	73	696	209
OLD FACTORY	99	20	9	797	704
RESTIGOUCHE	386	128	56	1822	1296
RIVER DESERT	680	226	62	1264	990
ROMAINE	6	0	0	646	645
ST-AUGUSTIN	0	0	0	130	127
TIMISKAMING	653	235	62	479	363
VIGER	96	13	1	125	8
WASKAGANISH	151	44	15	1307	1235
WASWANIPI	119	36	15	920	770
WEYMONTACHIE	55	11	10	694	661
WOLF LAKE	54	19	3	46	20
QUÉBEC - BANDES INCONNUES	224	4	0	0	0
TOTAL POUR LE QUÉBEC	9708	3527	1102	35074	29987
ONTARIO					
ALBANY	505	128	36	2011	1354
ALDERVILLE	657	195	33	242	134
AROLAND	14	6	6	226	17
ATTAWAPISKAT	194	55	17	1620	1010
BAIE GULL	101	30	12	464	348

NOM DE LA BANDE	NOMBRE TOTAL DE DEMANDES D'INSCRIPTION AU 87-05-31	NOMBRE TOTAL DES INSCRIPTIONS AU 87-05-31	NOMBRE TOTAL DE PERSONNES INSCRITES SUR LES LISTES DES BANDES AU 87-05-31	POPULATION INDIENNE INSCRITE JUIN 1985	POPULATION DES RÉSERVES JUIN 1985
BAIE WASHAGAMIS	19	6	2	140	102
BATCHEWANA	507	124	47	539	385
BEARFOOT ONONDAGA	67	33	11	317	186
BEARSKIN LAKE	54	10	6	462	389
BEAUSOLEIL	350	114	34	766	551
BIG GRASSY	60	7	2	312	207
BIG ISLAND	55	19	9	229	96
BRUNSWICK HOUSE	142	35	10	252	104
CALDWELL	16	6	2	79	0
CAT LAKE	0	0	0	377	371
CHAPLEAU CREE	134	28	7	40	5
CHIPPEWAS DE GEORGINA ISLAND	247	57	24	237	120
CHIPPEWAS DE KETTLE & STONY POINT	349	114	53	1052	732
CHIPPEWAS DE LA THAMES	219	77	34	1229	718
CHIPPEWAS DE NAWASH	549	193	50	934	532
CHIPPEWAS DE RAMA	397	94	40	551	369
CHIPPEWAS DE SARNIA	420	164	59	881	524
COUCHICHING	484	157	55	772	435
CURVE LAKE	467	135	32	817	607
DALLES	36	9	2	134	44
DEER LAKE	89	12	5	547	521
DELEWARE	139	46	12	340	183
DOKIS	308	79	18	306	166
EAGLE LAKE	53	19	5	182	137
FLYING POST	63	11	3	35	0
FORT HOPE	130	18	10	1246	848
FORT SEVERN	47	11	2	318	289
FORT WILLIAM	300	80	29	556	430
GARDEN RIVER	493	126	41	864	803
GIBSON	284	93	34	253	73
GOLDEN LAKE	483	127	53	585	272
GRASSY NARROWS	70	36	8	688	482
HENVEY INLET	85	40	2	209	120
HIAWATHA	223	34	11	150	91
ÎLE COCKBURN	29	2	2	33	9
ISLINGTON	41	15	6	901	644
KEE-WAY-WIN	0	0	0	366	300
KINGFISHER	8	4	0	277	276
KONADAHA SENECA	75	20	8	229	118
LAC BIG TROUT	98	20	6	758	735
LAC CARIBOU	51	24	12	520	509
LAC CONSTANCE	134	46	15	824	632
LAC DES MILLE LACS	142	48	19	99	3
LAC KASABONIKA	8	3	2	491	483
LAC LA CROIX	10	0	0	246	225
LAC LONG NO. 58	254	61	28	638	409
LAC LONG NO. 77	205	46	24	321	146
LAC McDOWELL	0	0	0	23	23

NOM DE LA BANDE	NOMBRE TOTAL DE DEMANDES D'INSCRIPTION AU 87-05-31	NOMBRE TOTAL DES INSCRIPTIONS AU 87-05-31	NOMBRE TOTAL DE PERSONNES INSCRITES SUR LES LISTES DES BANDES AU 87-05-31	POPULATION INDIENNE INSCRITE JUIN 1985	POPULATION DES RÉSERVES JUIN 1985
LAC MUSKRAT DAM	13	10	4	214	195
LAC SACHIGO	29	15	5	409	336
LAC SEUL	229	51	24	1384	664
LANSDOWNE HOUSE	0	0	0	178	178
LOWER CAYUGA	210	66	35	1771	1145
LOWER MOHAWK	475	184	70	1872	1176
MAGNETAWAN	60	14	4	84	36
MARTIN FALLS	38	9	6	289	203
MATACHEWAN	192	30	16	156	40
MATTAGAMI	76	11	6	170	103
MICHIPICOTEN	209	24	5	163	49
MISSANABIE CREE	90	22	1	73	3
MISSISSAUGA	274	75	31	406	328
MISSISSAUGAS DE NEW CREDIT	329	103	40	744	562
MOHAWKS DE AKWESASNE	675	105	36	4762	4404
MOHAWKS DE LA BAIE DE QUINTE	212	51	10	313	167
MOHAWKS DE LA BAIE DE QUINTE	2514	597	187	2822	1355
MOOSE FACTORY	562	172	48	1646	1097
MORAVIENS DE LA THAMES	185	34	10	556	354
MUNCEYS DE LA THAMES	81	9	6	251	135
NAICATCHEWENIN	13	2	1	203	173
NATION SAUGEEN	21	0	0	129	33
NEW POST	35	11	2	78	0
NEW SLATE FALLS	3	0	0	81	48
NICICKOUSEMENECANING	11	2	1	121	86
NIHARONDASA SENECA	67	16	6	191	86
NIPIGON	78	13	3	60	42
NIPISSING	731	214	65	694	490
NORTH SPIRIT LAKE	0	0	0	280	240
NORTHWEST ANGLE NO. 33	42	13	5	204	129
NORTHWEST ANGLE NO. 37	84	18	2	133	88
OJIBWAYS DE CHAPLEAU	7	0	0	22	22
OJIBWAYS D'ONEGAMING	57	7	2	374	250
ONEIDA	256	96	41	979	515
ONEIDAS DE LA THAMES	376	84	27	2736	1425
ONONDAGA CLEAR SKY	62	8	4	369	247
OSNABURGH	81	25	12	838	680
PARRY ISLAND	266	50	16	440	263
PAYS PLAT	82	33	6	92	72
PIC HERON BAY	202	36	13	418	317
PIC MOBERT	179	43	13	403	271
PIKANGIKUM	9	0	0	1180	1127
POINTE MOOSE DEER	80	14	9	163	78
POPLAR HILL	0	0	0	209	200
RAT PORTAGE	28	8	5	299	197
RED ROCK	437	146	38	379	144
RIVIÈRE WHITEFISH	175	45	18	444	271
RIVIÈRE-DE-LA-PLUIE	98	34	17	513	227

NOM DE LA BANDE	NOMBRE TOTAL DE DEMANDES D'INSCRIPTION AU 87-05-31	NOMBRE TOTAL DES INSCRIPTIONS AU 87-05-31	NOMBRE TOTAL DE PERSONNES INSCRITES SUR LES LISTES DES BANDES AU 87-05-31	POPULATION INDIENNE INSCRITE JUIN 1985	POPULATION DES RÉSERVES JUIN 1985
ROCKY BAY	111	48	21	300	229
SANDPOINT	76	12	1	39	16
SANDY LAKE	12	10	3	1262	1181
SAUGEEN	212	79	26	865	615
SCUGOG	45	4	2	50	23
SEINE RIVER	28	9	5	405	252
SERPENT RIVER	324	91	27	431	219
SHAWANAGA	160	24	10	152	81
SHEGUIANDAH	41	7	3	130	101
SHESHEGWANING	160	24	10	159	110
SHOAL LAKE NO. 39	53	14	6	316	243
SHOAL LAKE NO. 40	33	9	3	245	144
SIX-NATIONS-RIVIÈRE GRANDE	213	32	15	0	0
SPANISH RIVER	305	53	17	1217	907
STANGECOMING	11	1	1	42	26
SUCKER CREEK	109	9	3	294	236
SUCKER LAKE (AUPARAVANT)	7	1	0	0	0
SUMMER BEAVER	0	0	0	269	269
THESSALON	78	11	1	112	54
TIMAGAMI	125	26	11	206	114
TUSCARORA	390	99	34	967	584
UPPER CAYUGA	651	195	71	1378	796
UPPER MOHAWK	1029	342	125	2496	1578
WABAUSKANG	34	6	3	88	19
WABIGOON	87	5	4	164	76
WAHGOSHIG	27	1	0	63	1
WAHNAPITAE	18	2	0	19	6
WALKER MOHAWK	32	9	4	252	163
WALPOLE ISLAND	478	104	57	2156	1623
WAPEKEKA	0	0	0	231	231
WAWAKAPEWIN	13	2	2	2	2
WEBEQUIE	8	6	2	460	455
WEENUSK	26	4	1	274	159
WEST BAY	333	92	32	1105	653
WHITEFISH BAY	60	10	4	595	485
WHITEFISH LAKE	198	57	16	291	217
WHITESAND	80	19	9	432	274
WIKWEMIKONG	936	177	58	3579	2322
WUNNUMIN	1	0	0	334	330
ONTARIO - BANDES INCONNUES	569	7	0	0	0
TOTAL POUR L'ONTARIO	26871	6918	2375	78363	53312

NOM DE LA BANDE	NOMBRE TOTAL DE DEMANDES D'INSCRIPTION AU 87-05-31	NOMBRE TOTAL DES INSCRIPTIONS AU 87-05-31	NOMBRE TOTAL DE PERSONNES INSCRITES SUR LES LISTES DES BANDES AU 87-05-31	POPULATION INDIENNE INSCRITE JUIN 1985	POPULATION DES RÉSERVES JUIN 1985
MANITOBA					
BARREN LANDS	245	33	19	363	316
BERENS RIVER	205	48	15	1089	815
BIRDTAIL SIOUX	16	7	2	294	224
BLOODVEIN	47	15	5	571	463
BROKENHEAD	159	64	22	637	195
BUFFALO POINT	38	10	3	34	23
CHEMAHAWIN	182	15	13	528	406
CRANE RIVER	128	28	11	248	136
CROSS LAKE	547	153	44	2562	2136
DAKOTA PLAINS	2	0	0	185	117
DAKOTA TIPI	19	5	2	171	98
DAUPHIN RIVER	14	1	1	117	99
EBB AND FLOW	158	29	12	825	529
FAIRFORD	204	39	20	1077	793
FISHER RIVER	422	103	45	1441	869
FORT ALEXANDER	551	163	65	3054	1996
FORT CHURCHILL	73	20	11	434	251
FOX LAKE	115	38	11	384	255
GAMBLERS	56	12	2	41	21
GARDEN HILL	39	21	9	1989	1839
GOD'S LAKE	68	44	20	1232	987
GOD'S RIVER	5	0	0	303	293
GRAND RAPIDS	221	54	19	418	299
HOLLOW WATER	155	22	14	580	455
INDIAN BIRCH	14	4	1	167	133
JACKHEAD	47	4	4	357	196
KEESEEKOOWENIN	79	18	8	412	229
LAKE MANITOBA	89	20	15	760	542
LAKE ST. MARTIN	122	42	24	979	524
LITTLE BLACK RIVER	74	17	6	364	256
LITTLE GRAND RAPIDS	74	25	6	1032	902
LITTLE SASKATCHEWAN	109	43	22	402	265
LONG PLAIN	161	52	19	1232	545
MATHIAS COLOMB	118	29	7	1478	1289
MOOSE LAKE	245	13	8	385	341
NELSON HOUSE	420	142	55	2248	2057
NORTHLANDS	15	8	3	481	450
NORWAY HOUSE	495	208	62	2833	2433
OAK LAKE	26	7	3	382	270
OXFORD HOUSE	96	34	14	1213	1134
PEGUIS	979	258	80	2918	1672
PINE CREEK	410	69	28	847	488
POPLAR RIVER	47	17	6	620	591
RED SUCKER LAKE	17	1	1	425	407
ROLLING RIVER	47	14	9	444	259
ROSEAU RIVER	50	26	18	1101	584

ANNEXE B: STATISTIQUES POUR CHAQUE BANDE

NOM DE LA BANDE	NOMBRE TOTAL DE DEMANDES D'INSCRIPTION AU 87-05-31	NOMBRE TOTAL DES INSCRIPTIONS AU 87-05-31	NOMBRE TOTAL DE PERSONNES INSCRITES SUR LES LISTES DES BANDES AU 87-05-31	POPULATION INDIENNE INSCRITE JUIN 1985	POPULATION DES RÉSERVES JUIN 1985
SANDY BAY	454	108	36	2260	1695
SHAMATTAWA	64	11	4	656	628
SHOAL RIVER	233	28	8	643	411
SIOUX VALLEY	95	31	15	1220	770
SPLIT LAKE	366	124	29	1378	1142
ST. THERESA POINT	22	13	7	1655	1507
SWAN LAKE	65	23	14	666	255
THE PAS	706	140	46	1566	1359
VALLEY RIVER	129	27	15	569	265
WAR LAKE	3	0	0	82	27
WASAGAMACK	13	6	2	745	710
WATERHEN	171	29	11	515	325
WAYWAYSEECAPPO	96	32	9	1032	601
YORK FACTORY	174	47	14	454	298
MANITOBA - BANDES INCONNUES	141	0	0	0	0
TOTAL POUR LE MANITOBA	10135	2594	974	53098	39175

SASKATCHEWAN

AHTAHKAKOOP	267	72	29	1412	1113
BEARDY'S AND OKEMASIS	129	52	23	1412	864
BIG C	113	16	7	441	408
BIG RIVER	78	18	10	1366	1174
BLACK LAKE	87	31	8	821	806
BUFFALO RIVER	118	27	9	473	413
CANOE LAKE	267	112	31	549	461
CARRY THE KETTLE	138	56	18	1153	648
COTE	141	54	24	1624	884
COWESSESS	392	90	35	1543	494
CUMBERLAND HOUSE	259	24	6	345	226
DAY STAR	29	7	5	273	143
ENGLISH RIVER	164	68	25	566	478
FISHING LAKE	98	32	11	728	370
FLYING DUST	131	54	15	402	276
FOND DU LAC	125	45	14	829	583
GORDON	263	101	37	1450	961
ISLAND LAKE	13	4	2	533	468
JAMES SMITH	146	42	14	1479	1067
JOHN SMITH	184	54	26	575	380
JOSEPH BIGHEAD	7	2	0	433	351
KAHKEWISTAHAW	121	24	6	750	291
KEESEEKOOSE	131	31	18	959	465
KEY	97	22	11	560	173

NOM DE LA BANDE	NOMBRE TOTAL DE DEMANDES D'INSCRIPTION AU 87-05-31	NOMBRE TOTAL DES INSCRIPTIONS AU 87-05-31	NOMBRE TOTAL DE PERSONNES INSCRITES SUR LES LISTES DES BANDES AU 87-05-31	POPULATION INDIENNE INSCRITE JUIN 1985	POPULATION DES RÉSERVES JUIN 1985
KINISTINO	38	9	5	474	284
LAC LA HACHE	123	32	8	470	452
LAC LA RONGE	594	178	75	3221	2801
LITTLE BLACK BEAR	28	16	6	233	110
LITTLE PINE	55	25	11	886	576
LUCKY MAN	5	2	1	64	20
MAKWA SAHGAIEHCAN	12	3	3	662	534
MISTAWASIS	194	49	19	1031	559
MONTREAL LAKE	144	46	22	1469	1158
MOOSE WOODS	24	12	3	199	135
MOOSOMIN	104	34	8	706	458
MOSQUITO - GRIZZLY BEAR'S HEAD	16	6	2	685	433
MUSCOWPETUNG	151	41	13	642	325
MUSKEG LAKE	249	74	32	703	320
MUSKOWEKWAN	75	23	11	681	385
NIKANEET	17	0	0	181	111
NUT LAKE	44	6	3	1368	683
OCHAPOWACE	115	30	12	660	284
OKANESE	62	11	7	266	137
ONE ARROW	31	9	5	673	370
ONION LAKE	219	80	38	1867	1496
PASQUA	125	56	12	821	414
PEEPEEKISIS	267	141	40	1153	633
PELICAN LAKE	56	9	6	503	463
PETER BALLANTYNE	582	107	35	2735	2509
PIAPOT	51	14	6	980	432
POORMAN	39	6	4	1299	707
POUNDMAKER	62	26	11	705	460
RED EARTH	53	13	5	573	536
RED PHEASANT	228	77	13	847	468
SAKIMAY	147	37	18	722	189
SAULTEAUX	33	12	3	543	331
SHOAL LAKE OF THE CREE NATION	32	3	1	320	314
STANDING BUFFALO	85	23	8	689	384
STAR BLANKET	25	17	9	225	130
STURGEON LAKE	106	30	14	1145	915
SWEET GRASS	100	28	9	810	471
THUNDERCHILD	70	31	7	1119	614
TURNOR LAKE	75	19	6	159	148
WAHPETON	36	29	13	140	131
WATERHEN LAKE	111	20	8	788	525
WHITE BEAR	144	59	28	1389	730
WITCHEKAN LAKE	11	0	0	298	228
WOOD MOUNTAIN	60	7	4	78	35
SASKATCHEWAN - BANDES INCONNUES	138	1	0	0	0
TOTAL POUR LA SASKATCHEWAN	8434	2489	928	55858	36895

NOM DE LA BANDE	NOMBRE TOTAL DE DEMANDES D'INSCRIPTION AU 87-05-31	NOMBRE TOTAL DES INSCRIPTIONS AU 87-05-31	NOMBRE TOTAL DE PERSONNES INSCRITES SUR LES LISTES DES BANDES AU 87-05-31	POPULATION INDIENNE INSCRITE JUIN 1985	POPULATION DES RÉSERVES JUIN 1985
ALBERTA					
ALEXANDER	230	57	24	752	565
ALEXIS	85	27	8	761	558
BEAVER LAKE	219	44	19	320	236
BIGSTONE CREE	952	179	91	2073	1570
BLACKFOOT	217	103	37	3308	2174
BLOOD	294	119	49	6322	5256
BOYER RIVER	96	20	8	333	205
COLD LAKE FIRST NATIONS	396	118	56	1078	694
CREE	228	52	19	1071	622
DENE THA'	158	64	26	1444	1236
DRIFTPILE	453	100	39	816	453
DUNCAN'S	54	2	2	63	42
ENOCH	219	101	34	907	732
ERMINESKIN	292	102	38	1598	1292
FORT CHIPEWYAN	317	27	12	327	195
FORT McKAY	96	28	7	235	140
FORT McMURRAY	170	36	17	154	38
FROG LAKE	125	43	13	995	745
GROUARD	55	9	4	91	47
HEART LAKE	54	3	3	107	63
HORSE LAKE	238	22	9	194	127
JANVIER	67	19	10	278	188
KEHEWIN	141	39	14	907	695
LITTLE RED RIVER	150	45	13	1607	1427
LOUIS BULL	23	9	7	799	609
LUBICON LAKE	44	4	1	191	116
MICHEL (AUPARAVANT)	567	131	0	0	0
MONTANA	466	11	3	449	324
O'CHIESE	37	10	7	381	308
PAUL	72	28	9	914	656
PEIGAN	165	46	22	1977	1497
SADDLE LAKE	935	483	182	4206	2982
SAMSON	287	133	46	3069	2484
SARCEE	145	37	14	738	673
SAWRIDGE	324	43	6	38	18
STONEY (BEARSPAW)	1	0	0	826	792
STONEY (CHINIKI)	3	2	1	829	808
STONEY (GOODSTONEY)	9	5	2	887	827
STURGEON LAKE	447	50	26	887	551
SUCKER CREEK	586	155	49	715	335
SUNCHILD CREE	20	4	2	491	336
SWAN RIVER	369	65	20	277	137
TALLCREE	190	43	12	388	276

NOM DE LA BANDE	NOMBRE TOTAL DE DEMANDES D'INSCRIPTION AU 87-05-31	NOMBRE TOTAL DES INSCRIPTIONS AU 87-05-31	NOMBRE TOTAL DE PERSONNES INSCRITES SUR LES LISTES DES BANDES AU 87-05-31	POPULATION INDIENNE INSCRITE JUIN 1985	POPULATION DES RÉSERVES JUIN 1985
WHITEFISH LAKE	501	97	43	706	503
ALBERTA - BANDES INCONNUES	511	6	0	0	0
TOTAL POUR L'ALBERTA	11008	2721	1004	44509	33532
COLUMBIE-BRITANNIQUE					
ADAMS LAKE	71	15	9	395	311
AHOUSAHT	99	30	14	1097	564
AITCHELITZ	0	0	0	18	18
ALEXANDRIA	56	14	1	64	43
ALEXIS CREEK	31	5	3	443	347
ALKALI LAKE	71	17	6	406	351
ANAHAM	78	34	15	832	637
ANDERSON LAKE	60	8	4	141	78
ASHCROFT	88	33	8	85	44
BEECHER BAY	23	11	2	137	77
BELLA COOLA	122	27	16	851	620
BLUEBERRY RIVER	34	11	3	171	120
BONAPARTE	117	10	7	406	180
BOOTHROYD	28	2	1	181	94
BOSTON BAR	96	10	0	103	69
BRIDGE RIVER	36	4	4	207	117
BROMAN LAKE	20	10	2	102	56
BURNS LAKE	47	3	1	33	26
BURRARD	88	15	10	168	145
CAMPBELL RIVER	158	69	25	247	115
CANIM LAKE	24	1	0	360	307
CANOE CREEK	51	12	3	314	174
CANYON CITY	54	5	2	211	123
CAPE MUDGE	209	80	32	436	307
CAYOOSE CREEK	17	0	0	113	84
CHEAM	74	39	11	197	138
CHEHALIS	123	32	14	506	332
CHEMAINUS	78	25	11	600	489
CHESLATTA	22	3	2	149	107
CLAYOQUOT	23	3	1	461	247
COLDWATER	99	6	3	340	232
COLUMBIA LAKE	20	3	2	146	88
COMOX	83	38	13	92	66
COOK'S FERRY	64	26	10	171	88
COQUITLAM	25	0	0	18	4
COWICHAN	192	46	25	2069	1535
COWICHAN LAKE	5	1	0	8	8
DITIDAHT	31	11	5	284	137

ANNEXE B: STATISTIQUES POUR CHAQUE BANDE

NOM DE LA BANDE	NOMBRE TOTAL DE DEMANDES D'INSCRIPTION AU 87-05-31	NOMBRE TOTAL DES INSCRIPTIONS AU 87-05-31	NOMBRE TOTAL DE PERSONNES INSCRITES SUR LES LISTES DES BANDES AU 87-05-31	POPULATION INDIENNE INSCRITE JUIN 1985	POPULATION DES RÉSERVES JUIN 1985
DOIG RIVER	16	6	2	141	110
DOUGLAS	24	7	3	133	55
EHATTESAHT	4	0	0	118	61
ESQUIMALT	14	1	1	92	51
FORT GEORGE	122	20	11	93	68
FORT NELSON	101	35	19	359	253
FORT WARE	47	3	2	222	175
FOUNTAIN	67	11	4	566	364
FRASER LAKE	41	9	2	217	158
GITANMAAX	479	128	52	935	550
GITLAKDAMIX	148	50	21	1115	694
GITWANGAK	179	47	14	533	343
GLEN VOWELL	78	15	5	228	126
GWA'SALA - NAKWAXDA'XW	8	2	1	375	352
HAGWILGET	203	53	9	284	158
HALALT	17	6	2	142	72
HALFWAY RIVER	6	0	0	138	118
HARTLEY BAY	121	48	16	461	242
HEILTSUK	179	76	34	1385	1257
HESQUIAHT	20	0	0	423	52
HIGH BAR	67	1	0	9	0
HOMALCO	55	13	4	226	95
HOPE	47	1	1	195	89
INGENIKA	8	2	2	201	160
ISKUT	38	11	5	357	234
KAMLOOPS	168	37	17	481	347
KANAKA BAR	43	10	5	76	32
KATZIE	69	18	8	210	145
KINCOLITH	318	61	20	1112	420
KISPIOX	256	78	33	739	431
KITAMAAT	192	55	30	1062	644
KITASOO	15	2	1	311	265
KITKATLA	144	33	13	1006	497
KITSEGUKLA	135	52	19	498	360
KITSELAS	166	36	6	118	47
KITSUMKALUM	342	41	11	142	77
KITWANCOOL	55	20	6	373	276
KLAHOOSE	80	12	6	101	33
KLUSKUS	3	0	0	127	91
KWAKIUTL	90	32	10	296	141
KWAW-KWAW-A-PILT	0	0	0	25	16
KWA-WA-AINEUK	0	0	0	21	21
KWIAKAH	1	0	0	13	6
KWICKSUTAINEUK-AH-KWAW-AH-MISH	34	15	4	191	67
KYUQUOT	42	12	3	274	191
LAKAHAHMEN	117	13	6	118	42
LAKALZAP	77	15	8	940	382
LAKE BABINE	166	49	17	1114	801

NOM DE LA BANDE	NOMBRE TOTAL DE DEMANDES D'INSCRIPTION AU 87-05-31	NOMBRE TOTAL DES INSCRIPTIONS AU 87-05-31	NOMBRE TOTAL DE PERSONNES INSCRITES SUR LES LISTES DES BANDES AU 87-05-31	POPULATION INDIENNE INSCRITE JUIN 1985	POPULATION DES RÉSERVES JUIN 1985
LANGLEY	17	0	0	75	53
LAX KW'ALAAMS	491	197	54	1610	909
LILLOOET	81	15	9	133	88
LITTLE SHUSWAP LAKE	39	11	8	195	154
LOWER KOOTENAY	9	1	1	99	81
LOWER NICOLA	154	36	12	440	315
LOWER SIMILKAMEEN	59	24	6	229	178
LYACKSON	32	10	6	101	21
LYTTON	245	69	39	1082	765
MALAHAT	1	0	0	179	111
MAMALELEQALA-QWE'QWA'SOT'ENOX	35	21	11	213	49
MASSET	695	183	50	1248	625
MATSQUI	29	10	2	61	26
McLEOD LAKE	45	8	3	241	87
METLAKATLA	221	57	12	275	124
MORICETOWN	292	98	19	787	480
MOUNT CURRIE	60	17	5	1169	830
MOWACHAHT	8	5	1	306	163
MUSQUEAM	169	56	25	541	382
NANAIMO	163	43	21	658	424
NANOOSE	6	1	0	135	80
NAZKO	25	5	4	191	147
NECOSLIE	245	63	21	751	470
NEE-TAHI-BUHN	32	6	5	126	72
NEMAIAH VALLEY	17	6	3	255	221
NESKAINLITH	84	12	9	354	231
NEW WESTMINSTER	0	0	0	2	0
NICOMEN	6	0	0	68	40
NIMPKISH	280	110	38	959	633
NOOAITCH	15	7	2	106	63
NORTH THOMPSON	102	18	8	355	179
NUCHATLAHT	0	0	0	89	41
OHAMIL	29	2	2	65	25
OHIAHT	28	12	4	335	101
OKANAGAN	354	144	58	895	603
OPETCHESAHT	33	22	11	120	56
OREGON JACK CREEK	3	1	1	26	11
OSOYOOS	43	7	3	175	158
OWEEKENO	41	7	3	152	65
PACHEENAHT	20	5	3	173	66
PAUQUACHIN	6	2	1	203	160
PAVILION	58	15	5	264	217
PENELAKUT	70	8	3	478	292
PENTICTON	94	20	12	397	303
PETERS	33	11	5	40	29
POPKUM	4	0	0	7	7
PROPHET RIVER	4	1	0	130	88
QUALICUM	20	1	1	47	37

NOM DE LA BANDE	NOMBRE TOTAL DE DEMANDES D'INSCRIPTION AU 87-05-31	NOMBRE TOTAL DES INSCRIPTIONS AU 87-05-31	NOMBRE TOTAL DE PERSONNES INSCRITES SUR LES LISTES DES BANDES AU 87-05-31	POPULATION INDIENNE INSCRITE JUIN 1985	POPULATION DES RÉSERVES JUIN 1985
QUATSINO	15	2	2	187	140
QUESNEL	17	1	1	68	59
SAMAHQUAM	31	7	3	154	1
SAULTEAU	160	29	14	203	135
SCOWLITZ	3	0	0	167	90
SEABIRD ISLAND	49	2	2	371	247
SECHELT	133	27	18	644	414
SEMIAHMOO	39	11	4	28	24
SETON LAKE	30	1	1	408	302
SHACKAN	8	3	1	92	54
SHESHAHT	64	40	13	517	436
SHUSWAP	44	3	2	150	99
SISKA	37	1	0	117	43
SKAWAHLOOK	5	0	0	54	16
SKEETCHESTN	77	14	7	253	134
SKIDEGATE	560	163	59	468	249
SKOOKUM CHUCK	38	9	6	230	28
SKOWKALE	8	0	0	94	69
SKUPPAH	28	5	3	31	18
SKWAH	68	9	5	263	141
SKWAY	25	2	2	46	11
SLIAMMON	57	13	12	518	443
SODA CREEK	48	13	9	173	121
SONGHEES	23	11	4	214	154
SOOKE	41	7	4	50	25
SOOWAHLIE	32	6	4	161	80
SPALLUMCHEEN	89	21	10	378	257
SPUZZUM	84	20	2	49	17
SQUAMISH	658	188	89	1531	1335
SQUIALA	5	0	0	71	48
STELLAQUO	108	13	4	206	154
STONE	4	1	1	210	186
STONY CREEK	99	29	10	463	356
STUART - TREMBLEUR LAKE	129	25	11	978	694
ST. MARY'S	59	13	2	152	108
SUMAS	43	18	6	136	109
TAHLTAN	653	125	33	534	185
TAKLA LAKE	73	17	3	385	274
TANAKTEUK	26	3	3	110	13
TLATLASIKWALA	0	0	0	27	10
TLOWITSIS - MUMTAGILA	26	5	3	172	51
TOBACCO PLAINS	33	2	1	87	75
TOOSEY	22	12	4	129	89
TOQUAHT	13	9	3	74	11
TSARTLIP	47	4	4	455	349
TSAWATAINEUK	73	21	7	308	118
TSAWOUT	70	15	6	359	265
TSAWWASSEN	79	26	9	63	44

NOM DE LA BANDE	NOMBRE TOTAL DE DEMANDES D'INSCRIPTION AU 87-05-31	NOMBRE TOTAL DES INSCRIPTIONS AU 87-05-31	NOMBRE TOTAL DE PERSONNES INSCRITES SUR LES LISTES DES BANDES AU 87-05-31	POPULATION INDIENNE INSCRITE JUIN 1985	POPULATION DES RÉSERVES JUIN 1985
TSEYCUM	11	5	4	101	61
TZEACHTEN	73	20	9	138	103
UCHUCKLESAHT	5	3	1	108	17
UCLUELET	35	10	3	396	274
ULKATCHO	56	12	5	419	337
UNION BAR	45	4	1	49	12
UPPER NICOLA	148	40	20	472	337
UPPER SIMILKAMEEN	6	0	0	30	23
WEST MOBERLY LAKE	24	2	1	72	26
WESTBANK	64	34	18	242	206
WHISPERING PINES	21	3	2	47	40
WILLIAMS LAKE	87	10	8	267	178
YAKWEAKWIOOSE	4	0	0	25	19
YALE	24	0	0	91	39
COLUMBIE-BRITANNIQUE - BANDES INCONNUES	324	2	0	0	0
TOTAL POUR LA COLOMBIE-BRITANNIQUE	16582	4233	1643	62393	39860

TERRITOIRES DU NORD-OUEST

NOM DE LA BANDE					
AKLAVIK	56	12	6	248	239
ARCTIC RED RIVER	75	14	6	253	239
DOG RIB RAE	147	31	16	1811	1748
FITZ-SMITH (ALTA - NWT) NATIVE	168	20	8	368	334
FORT FRANKLIN	45	16	8	546	527
FORT GOOD HOPE	107	19	5	482	473
FORT LIARD	54	4	4	493	479
FORT McPHERSON	302	67	30	724	701
FORT NORMAN	115	13	3	236	228
FORT PROVIDENCE	76	15	5	630	580
FORT SIMPSON	130	34	11	762	725
FORT WRIGLEY	29	9	7	216	211
HAY RIVER	64	5	3	303	283
INUVIK NATIVE	20	0	0	94	2
RESOLUTION	143	6	3	380	345
SNOWDRIFT	28	5	1	331	292
YELLOWKNIFE 'B'	74	16	6	648	575
T.N.-O. - BANDES INCONNUES	57	0	0	0	0
TOTAL POUR LES TERRITOIRES DU NORD-OUEST	1690	286	128	8525	7981

NOM DE LA BANDE	NOMBRE TOTAL DE DEMANDES D'INSCRIPTION AU 87-05-31	NOMBRE TOTAL DES INSCRIPTIONS AU 87-05-31	NOMBRE TOTAL DE PERSONNES INSCRITES SUR LES LISTES DES BANDES AU 87-05-31	POPULATION INDIENNE INSCRITE JUIN 1985	POPULATION DES RÉSERVES JUIN 1985
YUKON					
AISHIHIK	46	25	10	86	56
CARCROSS-TAGISH	220	61	12	145	104
CHAMPAGNE	186	66	24	175	105
DAWSON	194	66	22	222	137
KLUANE	163	38	10	110	80
KWANLIN DUN	313	140	34	543	482
LIARD RIVER	140	34	15	620	474
LITTLE SALMON - CARMACKS	85	31	13	301	228
NA-CHO NY'A'K-DUN	122	63	29	224	204
OLD CROW	113	51	18	236	179
ROSS RIVER	36	20	8	289	270
SELKIRK	172	21	10	287	169
TAKU RIVER TLINGIT	159	33	11	187	73
TESLIN	171	51	21	265	211
TOTAL POUR LE YUKON	2120	700	237	3690	2772
REGION - BANDES INCONNUES	163	0	0	0	0
TOTAL POUR LE CANADA	90051	24708	8791	355321	253499

ANNEXE C

BANDES ET ASSOCIATIONS BÉNÉFICIANT D'UN
FINANCEMENT POUR L'ÉLABORATION DE RÈGLES D'APPARTENANCE
AU 31 MAI 1987.

Le total des fonds fournis aux bandes et aux associations pour l'élaboration de règles d'appartenance s'élevait, le 31 mai 1987, à 3 604 272 $.

La répartition de ces fonds par région était la suivante :

RÉGION DE L'ATLANTIQUE   TOTAL DES FONDS FOURNIS : 163 500 $

BANDES RECEVANT DES FONDS :

ABEGWEIT	EEL RIVER	PAPINEAU
BIG COVE	ESKASONI	RED BANK
BUCTOUCHE	FORT FOLLY	SAINT MARY'S
BURNT CHURCH	INDIAN ISLAND	SHUBENACADIE
CHAPEL ISLAND	LENNOX ISLAND	VALLÉE D'ANNAPOLIS
EDMUNDSTON	MILLBROOK	WAGAMATCOOK
EEL GROUND	OROMOCTO	WHYCOCOMAGH
		WOODSTOCK

RÉGION DU QUÉBEC   TOTAL DES FONDS FOURNIS : 187 900 $

BANDES RECEVANT DES FONDS :

ABÉNAKIS DE WOLINAK	MONTAGNAIS DE SEPT-ÎLES ET
ABITIBIWINNI	MALIOTENAM
BETSIAMITES	MONTAGNAIS DE NATASHQUAN
GASPÉ	MONTAGNAIS DU LAC ST-JEAN
KAHNAWAKE	NATION HURONNE WENDAT
KANESATAKE	OBEDJIWAN
KIPAWA	ODANAK
LAC SIMON	RESTIGOUCHE
LONG POINT	RIVER DESERT
MANOUANE	TIMISKAMING
MICMACS DE MARIA	WEYMONTACHIE
MINGAN	WOLF LAKE

ANNEXE C

BANDES ET ASSOCIATIONS BÉNÉFICIANT D'UN
FINANCEMENT POUR L'ÉLABORATION DE RÈGLES D'APPARTENANCE
AU 31 MAI 1987

RÉGION DE L'ONTARIO   **TOTAL DES FONDS FOURNIS : 776 392 $**

ALDERVILLE	MOHAWKS DE LA BAIE DE QUINTE
AROLUND	POINTE MOOSE DEER
BEAUSOLEIL	MOOSE FACTORY
BIG GRASSY	MUNCEYS DE LA THAMES
BIG ISLAND	NAICATCHEWENIN
LAC BIG TROUT	NICICKOUSEMENECANING
CALDWELL	NIPISSING
CHIPPEWAS DE GEORGINA ISLAND	NORTHWEST ANGLE No 33
CHIPPEWAS DE KETTLE ET STONY POINT	NORTHWEST ANGLE No 37
CHIPPEWAS DE NAWASH	OJIBWAYS D'ONEGAMING
CHIPPEWAS DE RAMA	ONEIDAS DE LA THAMES
CHIPPEWAS DE SARNIA	PARRY ISLAND
CHIPPEWAS DE LA THAMES	PAYS PLAT
ÎLE COCKBURN	PIC HERON BAY
LAC CONSTANCE	PIC MOBERT
COUCHICHING	PIKANGIKUM
CURVE LAKE	RAT PORTAGE
DALLES	RIVIÈRE-DE-LA-PLUIE
DEER LAKE	RIVIÈRE WHITEFISH
DOKIS	ROCKY BAY
EAGLE LAKE	SANDPOINT
FORT HOPE	SCUGOG
FORT WILLIAM	SEINE RIVER
GARDEN RIVER	SHAWANAGA
GIBSON	SHEGUIANDAH
GRASSY NARROWS	SHOAL LAKE No 39
BAIE GULL	SIX-NATIONS - GRAND RIVER
HENVEY INLET	STANGECOMING
HIAWATHA	SUCKER CREEK
ISLINGTON	WABIGOON
LAC DES MILLE LACS	WAHCOSHIG
LAC LA CROIX	WAHNAPITAE
LAC SEUL	WALPOLE ISLAND
LONG LAKE No 58	WAPENEKE
LONG LAKE No 77	WASHEGAMIS BAY
MAGNETAWAN	WHITEFISH BAY
MISSISSAUGA	WHITESAND
MISSISSAUGAS DE NEW CREDIT	WIKWEMIKONG
MOHAWKS D'AKWESASNE	

ASSOCIATIONS AUTOCHTONES RECEVANT DES FONDS :

CONSEIL TRIBAL DE LA CÔTE NORD
CONSEIL DU SECTEUR DE PEHTABUN
CONSEIL TRIBAL SHIBOGAMA
CONSEIL DU SECTEUR DE WINDIGO

BANDES ET ASSOCIATIONS BÉNÉFICIANT D'UN
FINANCEMENT POUR L'ÉLABORATION DE RÈGLES D'APPARTENANCE
AU 31 MAI 1987

RÉGION DU MANITOBA   TOTAL DES FONDS FOURNIS : 309 100 $

BARREN LANDS	LAKE MANITOBA	ROSEAU RIVER
CRANE RIVER	LAKE ST. MARTIN	SANDY BAY
CROSS LAKE	LITTLE SASKATCHEWAN	SIOUX VALLEY
DAKOTA TIPI	LONG PLAIN	SPLIT LAKE
EBB AND FLOW	NELSON HOUSE	SWAN LAKE
FAIRFORD	NORWAY HOUSE	VALLEY RIVER
FISHER RIVER	OAK LAKE	WATERHEN
FORT ALEXANDER	OXFORD HOUSE	WAYWAYSEECAPPO
GAMBLERS	PEGUIS	WASAGAMACK
GOD'S LAKE	PINE CREEK	YORK FACTORY

ASSOCIATIONS AUTOCHTONES RECEVANT DES FONDS :

CONSEIL DE DÉVELOPEMENT DE LA RÉGION DU SUD-EST
CONSEIL TRIBAL D'ISLAND LAKE

RÉGION DE LA SASKATCHEWAN   TOTAL DES FONDS FOURNIS : 463 000 $

AHTAHKAKOOP	KEY	PEEPEEKISIS
BEARDY'S & OKEMASIS	KINISTINO	PELICAN LAKE
BIG C	LAC LA HACHE	PETER BALLANTYNE
BIG RIVER	LITTLE BLACK BEAR	PIAPOT
BLACK LAKE	LITTLE PINE	POUNDMAKER
BUFFALO RIVER	LUCKY MAN	RED EARTH
CANOE LAKE	MAKWA SAHGAIEHCAN	RED PHEASANT
CARRY THE KETTLE	MISTAWASIS	SAKIMAY
COTE	MONTREAL LAKE	SAULTEAUX
COWESSESS	MOOSE WOODS	SHOAL LAKE
CUMBERLAND HOUSE	MOOSOMIN	STANDING BUFFALO
FISHING LAKE	MUCKEG LAKE	STAR BLANKET
JAMES SMITH	NIKANEET	STURGEON LAKE
JOSEPH BIGHEAD	NUT LAKE	SWEET GRASS
JOHN SMITH	OCHAPOWACE	THUNDERCHILD
KAHKEWISTAHAW	OKANESE	WAHPETON
KEESEEKOOSE	ONION LAKE	WHITE BEAR
		WITCHEKAN LAKE

ASSOCIATIONS AUTOCHTONES RECEVANT DES FONDS :

MEADOW LAKE DISTRICT CHIEF MANAGEMENT COMPANY LIMITED

BANDES ET ASSOCIATIONS BÉNÉFICIANT D'UN
FINANCEMENT POUR L'ÉLABORATION DE RÈGLES D'APPARTENANCE
AU 31 MAI 1987

RÉGION DE L'ALBERTA   **TOTAL DES FONDS FOURNIS : 266 500 $**

BANDES RECEVANT DES FONDS :

ALEXANDER	ERMINESKIN	PEIGAN
ALEXIS	FORT CHIPEWYAN	SADDLE LAKE
BEAVER LAKE	FORT McKAY	SARCEE
BIGSTONE CREE	FORT McMURRAY	STONEY(CHINIKI)
BLACKFOOT	HEART LAKE	STURGEON LAKE
BLOOD	HORSE LAKE	SUCKER LAKE
COLD LAKE FIRST NATIONS	JANVIER	SUNCHILD CREE
CREE	LITTLE RED RIVER	SWAN RIVER
DENE THA'	LUBICON LAKE	TALLCREE
DRIFTPILE	O'CHIESE	WHITEFISH LAKE
ENOCH	PAUL	

RÉGION DE LA COLOMBIE-BRITANNIQUE   **TOTAL DES FONDS FOURNIS : 1 276 880 $**

BANDES RECEVANT DES FONDS :

ADAMS LAKE	KITAMAAT	PENELAKUT
ALEXANDRIA	KITKATLA	PENTICTON
ANAHAM	KITSEGUKLA	QUALICUM
ASHCROFT	KITSELAS	QUATSINO
BELLA COOLA	KITSUMKALUM	QUESNEL
BONAPARTE	KITWANCOOL	SAMAHQUAM
BOSTON BAR	KWAKIUTL	SAULTEAU
BURRARD	LAKALZAP	SCOWLITZ
CAMPBELL RIVER	LAX KW'ALAAMS	SETON LAKE
CANIM LAKE	LILLOOET	SKEETCHESIN
CANOE CREEK	LITTLE SHUSWAP LAKE	SKIDEGATE
CANYON CITY	LOWER SIMILKAMEEN	SKWAH
CAPE MUDGE	LYTTON	SODA CREEK
CHEMAINUS	MALAHAT	SONGHEES
COOK'S FERRY	MASSET	SPALLUMCHEEN
DOIG RIVER	McLEOD LAKE	SOUAMISH
GITANMAAX	METLAKATLA	STELLAQUO
GITLAKDAMIX	MORICETON	THALTON
GLEN VOWELL	MUSQUEAM	TABACCO PLAINS
HAGWILGET	NANAIMO	TSARTLIP
HARTLEY BAY	NANOOSE	TSAWOUT
HOMALCO	NAZKO	TSAWWASSEN
KAMLOOPS	NORTH THOMPSON	TSEYCUM
KATZIE	OHIAHT	UPPER SIMILKAMEEN
KINCOLITH	OSOYOOSAHT	WESTBANK
KISPIOX	PACHEENAHT	WHISPERING PINES
	PAUQUACHIN	WILLIAMS LAKE

BANDES ET ASSOCIATIONS BÉNÉFICIANT D'UN
FINANCEMENT POUR L'ÉLABORATION DE RÈGLES D'APPARTENANCE
AU 31 MAI 1987

ASSOCIATIONS AUTOCHTONES RECEVANT DES FONDS :

CONSEIL TRIBAL DES CARRIERS-SEKANIS
CONSEIL TRIBAL DE DESOLATION SOUND
CONSEIL DES INDIENS DU SECTEUR DE KOOTENAY
ADMINISTRATION INDIENNE DE LA VALLÉE DE LA NICOLA
CONSEIL TRIBAL DE LA NATION NLAKA'PAMUX
CONSEIL TRIBAL NUU-CHAH-NULTH
SOCIÉTÉ DA LA NATION STO:LO
ASSOCIATIONS DES TRIBUS ASSUJETTIES AU TRAITÉ N° 8

RÉGION DU YUKON   TOTAL DES FONDS FOURNIS : 90 000 $

BANDES RECEVANT DES FONDS :

CARCROSS-TAGISH	LITTLE SALMON-CARMACES
CHAMPAGNE	NA-CHOW NY'A'K-DUN
DAWSON	OLD CROW
KLUANE	SELKIRK
KWANLIN DUN	TAKU RIVER TLINGIT
LIARD RIVER	TESLIN

RÉGION DES TERRITOIRES DU NORD-OUEST   TOTAL DES FONDS FOURNIS : 25 500 $

BANDES RECEVANT DES FONDS :

FORT LIARD
FORT McPHERSON
INUVIK NATIVE

D'autres associations autochtones non encore indiquées ont bénéficié d'une somme supplémentaire de 45 500 $ pour l'élaboration de leurs règles d'appartenance.

ANNEXE D

BANDES PRÉSENTANT DES RÈGLES D'APPARTENANCE

Bandes administrant leur effectif au 31 mai 1987 :

RÉGION	NOM DE LA BANDE	DATES D'ENTRÉE EN VIGUEUR DES RÈGLES
Ontario	Chippewas de Georgina Island	27 févr. 1987
	Wapekeka	15 juill. 1987
Saskatchewan	Cumberland House	16 sept. 1985
Alberta	Driftpile	9 nov. 1986
	Ermineskin	2 juill. 1986
	Fort McMurray	2 janv. 1987
	Horse Lake	3 juin 1986
	Lubicon Lake	3 févr. 1986
	Sawridge	8 juill. 1985
	Swan River	4 avril 1986
Colombie-Britannique	Saulteau	17 nov. 1986
	Sechelt	19 sept. 1985

Autres bandes ayant fait parvenir leurs règles d'appartenance au ministre au 31 mai 1987 :

RÉGION	NOM DE LA BANDE	DATES DE RÉCEPTION
Atlantique	Buctouche	*
	Miawpukek	*
Québec	Abénakis de Wolinak	mai 1987
Ontario	Big Island	avril 1987
	Lac McDowell	mars 1987
	Moose Deer Point	mai 1987
	North Spirit Lake	mars 1987
	Pays Plat	avril 1987
	Sandy Lake	mars 1987
	Whitesand	déc. 1986

ANNEXE D

Manitoba	Buffalo Point	mars 1987
	Crane River	mai 1987
	Lake St. Martin	août 1986
Saskatchewan	Saulteaux	mai 1987
Alberta	Alexander	mai 1987
	Beaver Lake	*
	Enoch	mai 1987
	Heart Lake	*
	Janvier	mai 1987
	Kehewin	*
	Sucker Creek	mai 1986
	Sunchild Cree	mai 1987
	Tallcree	avril 1987
Colombie-Britannique	Alexandria	avril 1987
	Burrard	mai 1987
	Canim Lake	avril 1987
	Glen Vowell	avril 1987
Yukon	Aishihik	avril 1987
	Champagne	avril 1987

Au 31 mai 1987, trois bandes avaient décidé de laisser au Ministère la gestion de leur liste de bande; il s'agit des bandes Afton, Horton, Pictou Landing (toutes trois de la Région de l'Atlantique).

* Les renseignements ont été reçus par le Ministère, mais il a fallu les renvoyer aux bandes afin de clarifier certains aspects ou de modifier certaines parties. Une fois ces changements effectués, les bandes pourront faire une nouvelle demande.